FUCKED + JOLLY
Ten Years of the Exponential Festival

edited by Nic Adams
introduction by Theresa Buchheister

Nic Adams | Tristan Allen | Leonie Bell | Eliza
Bent | Theresa Buchheister | Ann Marie Dorr |
Salomé Egas | Lena Engelstein | Shawn Escar-
ciga | Lisa Fagan | David Greenspan | Ben
Holbrook | Hannah Kallenbach | Kate Kremer
| Sleth | Joey Merlo | Nicolás Noreña | Kyoung
Park | Cristina Pitter | Lee Rayment | Evan
Silver | Marissa Joyce Stamps | Cameron Stu-
art | Cristina Tang | Alex Tatarsky | Sanaz B
Tennent | Ellpetha Tsivicos | Bailey Williams

53 SP 51

Fucked + Jolly: Ten Years of the Exponential Festival
© Nic Adams 2024
53rdstatepress.org

ISBN Number: 979-8986581460
Library of Congress Control Number: 2024944687

Book design: Kate Kremer
Cover design: Mark Toneff

Printed on recycled paper in the United States of America.

Fucked + Jolly is made possible by the New York State Council on the Arts with the support of the Office of the Governor and the New York State Legislature.

FUCKED + JOLLY
Ten Years of the Exponential Festival

edited by Nic Adams
introduction by Theresa Buchheister

53rd State Press
Brooklyn, NY

CONTENTS

INTRODUCTION

Thank goodness Kate Kremer approved the name that makes the absolute most sense for this book—*Fucked + Jolly*. All meanings of Fucked. All meanings of Jolly. And and.

We (here at The Exponential Festival) love sense. Everything in this book makes sense. Making sense does not mean we are not in the practice of melting minds.

Ever since The Exponential Festival birthed itself into existence, the mindset has been: "If it stops feeling necessary and stops being fun, we will stop doing it." That does not mean it is easy. That does not mean it isn't work. It means that the struggle and the labor fuel the joy and the substance. It means we live always in the micro and the macro, the post mortem and the act of creation, the ridiculous and the constrained.

As we reflect on the past ten years of Exponential-ing, let's start by going back in time...

In 2015, an "anonymous" letter to CultureBot regarding the January festivals had made the rounds, my company Title:Point had been doing "theater" in the DIY venue Silent Barn for three years, The Ontological had been gutted and turned into a ballet school for rich girls, and everyone I knew was broke. So, when Object Collection asked to do a one-night special showing in the recording studio (Gravesend) at Silent Barn in January with the hopes of the weirdest of the APAP attendees checking them out, I said, "Yes. Is a door split cool? What all do you need?"

The show was unforgettable. I had to keep running over to

Kara Feely to ask if the playing space could reduce because more people wanted to get in. By the time we started, audience was sitting with their knees practically touching the central table, the door to Stanwix could not open to allow anyone else in, and Daniel Nelson was up in the little pig loft where the drum kit was stashed, probably thinking, "Wow. My blocking is going to be a bit different than planned." Shortly after this one fun night, Title:Point did a month-long run of *Biter (Every Time I Turn Around)* and Eliza Bent did a month-long run of *Toilet Fire*.

Tale as old as time, due to our shows running simultaneously, we missed out on each other's art. We met to lament this and tell stories in my apartment on 5th between 2nd and 3rd that I shared with DJ Mendel, me chain smoking out the window (DJ already did, so no point in me not following suit), Eliza and me sipping bourbon. We both loved our shows. We both had received solid reactions (thanks, Helen Shaw). We both wanted to share this art we were so proud of with each other. So, perhaps a little in our cups, I proposed we do our shows again in January, because Object Collection did their show in January and it went so well. Then I could see hers and she could see mine.

Now, a lot happened after that but this here piece of writing is an introduction to this book of collected conversations/interviews with Exponential Festival artists, not a history of every little thing that happened between January 2015 and now. HOWEVER, I will totally write that history or make that documentary if anyone wants to collaborate. Give me a call. For now, I will let the story of these beginnings create a little stage for these big ideas to dance around on.

Whose ideas, you ask? Well, The Exponential Festival has featured hundreds of artists over the years. We have crammed into the tiniest of spaces and spread out into the wide world of digital space. I personally have watched a show through a window while it was snowing because it was too crowded inside; I've seen a performer's fingernail get hole punched by an audience member; I've performed a matinee in Sunset Park, loaded out, raced to Williamsburg for an 8pm comedy double bill and then to East Williamsburg for a 10pm show for an audience of two performed by one actor who created lighting looks with paper on an overhead projector and piped the soundtrack into my earbuds and over the sound system, all on the day of the Full Wolf Moon. I have rarely missed an Exponential show, though I made it impossible for myself to see 100%. Over these ten years, I willfully have broken apart my "understanding" of art, artists, and "how to do things" and have absorbed all of the magic that came pouring out of the people who have made this festival "the bleeding edge" of NY performance.

Now for a fun exercise and then on to reading these brilliant conversations! I will write a memory of a performance by each contributor, to prove (even though nobody is asking) that what these artists have shared STICKS. To the brain. To the soul. To the memory. To the very atmosphere.

Lisa Fagan—A dirt-covered gleeful leap through a ten-foot-tall pile of spray-painted boxes.

Shawn Escarciga—Little pride flags in their butt and Marina wig on head.

Evan Silver—The tenderness of Echo in *Cryptochrome* at The Cell, filling the space and minds vibrating in time together.

Christina Tang—The beautiful chaos of the final minutes of *TRAFFIC*.

Tristan Allen—The exquisite moments of world expansion when Tin Iso leaves the frame and another when Tristan returns to piano.

David Greenspan—The delicate and precise "cigarette" choreo of *Theda Bara*. And the pronunciation of "Google."

Sleth—Tulsa Swinton red wine extravaganza.

Cameron Stuart—The transformation of entire vibe with the donning of an epic wig.

Ben Holbrook—Soothing sweet dad chuckle in *Arrow of Time*.

Sanaz B Tennent—Aerobics routine with martini in the 2019 ?!:New Works.

Theresa Buchheister (ME!)—Getting doused in a gallon of stage blood by my brother aka Chris R as Justin Anselmi aka Mark and Averyn Mackey aka Lisa weep on my crotch in our performance of *The Room*.

Lena Engelstein—The rotating and pulsing circle of high kicks in *Community Exercises for Sanctuary Spaces*… or chugging a beer after sprinting and leaping into another performer's arms in *1-800-3592113592*.

Eliza Bent—The very first night I met Eliza for real for real at a Banana Bag and Bodice fundraiser where she talked about her gastrointestinal experiences, which would become *Toilet Fire*.

Joey Merlo—The rapt focus of the audience during the pitch

black scene in *On Set with Theda Bara*, listening so intently. What a thrill!

Cristina Pitter—An eternal feeling, which is a holding—of space, of me, of time, of energy. And a moment, when I first heard Cristina's voice enter the world of *BLOODSHOT*.

Bailey Williams—A very culty performance at Little Theater at Dixon Place. I was like—Sign me up!

Leonie Bell—In the backroom of Crystal Lake, Leonie made the wildest salad mess I have ever seen and it was glorious.

Lee Rayment—Honestly, Kermit singing *Les Mis*. It was everything.

Salomé Egas—A packed-to-the-gills room at Para//el, watching through a mirror's reflection, paint in more places than perhaps planned.

Ellpetha Tsivicos—Shooting *Night Descends on Svalbard* at The Brick. The moon. THE MOON. It was magic.

Hannah Kallenbach—The list is long with this one. But the very first performance of Hannah's that I saw was at SalOn! and they sat atop an ice dildo that they had made and placed atop a huge traffic cone that they had "found" and painted silver... and then delivered a searing monologue to a goldfish in a bowl. Also, Hannah donated their hand sanitizing machine to The Brick so that we could open the space to protestors. That machine featured in many of their performances and videos. Also, the November 2016 SalOn! at Footlight, where Hannah processed the election.

Nicolás Noreña—Again, too many for this introduction...

but I would say, the psychic communication that led to me pouring seltzer in Nico's mouth at Roly Polies OR the multiple runway trips in *Those Movable Pieces* OR the muffin halos on the angel ramp in *LAPA*...OR his butt in *The Passerby*.

Kyoung Park—Meeting with Kyoung at Veselka before the pandemic to discuss the possibilities of his expansive mind.

Alex Tatarsky—Alex realizing there was a young child in the audience at The Hole, as they pulled a banana out of their pants.

Ann Marie Dorr—"May I ask you for a kindness" will live with me forever. And also the cookies followed by karaoke in *Good and Noble Beings*.

Kate Kremer—The first show I saw in new JACK, moved and, honestly, pretty emotional.

Nic Adams—Seeing Nic do *Icarus*. So beautiful. Seeing Nic deal with Peter Mills Weiss as the tech person at the longest SalOn! in history. lol.

Marissa Joyce Stamps—Talking about how to bring a boxing ring into The Brick. It happening. The patient and deep beauty of *Blue Fire Burns the Hottest*.

—Theresa Buchheister, September 2024

LISA FAGAN + SHAWN ESCARCIGA

LISA FAGAN *first presented her work with The Exponential Festival in 2019. The piece was called* Red Carrots *and featured many collaborators who would go on to present their work at the festival. The next year, Fagan became Exponential's inaugural Artistic Fellow, creating and premiering a new piece,* Catches No Flies, *in 2020.*

That same year, SHAWN ESCARCIGA *first presented with Exponential a piece entitled* Very Real and Legitimate MFA Thesis Show from an Accredited University. *Escarciga would go on to present* ADMIN REVEAL, *a live show based on their meme account @missladysalad on Instagram.*

LISA FAGAN. I don't think we've ever even met.

SHAWN ESCARCIGA. No, I don't think so.

LF. And I've heard your name.

SE. I've heard your name. I knew who you were.

LF. And I actually don't think I've ever done something like this before.

SE. I don't think I have either.

LF. You said that your work is like "Applebee's Times Square and birds." You have no idea how much that resonated with me. I was like, "What is it in that description that is so specifically compelling to me?" So maybe that's my first question. What is that for you?

SE. I feel like Applebee's Times Square is this kind of kitschy, nostalgic thing that I also secretly like—it's not a secret. And it's also something that is just kind of silly. I don't know. There's something kind of interesting about places that you're not *supposed* to like—but you *are* supposed to like—and then you return to them. I grew up going to Applebee's. But later I was like, "I don't want to go Times Square or Applebee's, but I *do* want to go to the Applebee's *in* Times Square."

LF. Yeah, and I just happen to be passing through Times Square—

SE. Or actively planning.

LF. —to boot.

SE. Oh, you just were?

LF. I constantly am—

SE. Yeah.

LF. So if I'm gonna go to an Applebee's—

SE. It's gonna be *that* one. Or that Shake Shack? And then birds, I don't know how I got into birds. And it's—I'm finding—a more progressively niche thing that people who like birds *really* like birds.

LF. That's super true. Ornithology club.

SE. And I'm not *quite* there yet. But I can feel it in my bones.

LF. Yeah, there's something about like—when you add birds on top of Applebee's, you get a third thing—

SE. Yep.

LF. —which is very...there's a flavor to it that I could match to some of the imagery that I was seeing in your work.

SE. That's a compliment.

LF. I felt it deeply. It is a little devastating that I've never seen your work. It's a product of a larger problem—how do we see everything? How do we see each other's work enough?

SE. When I was watching your work, I was like, "I really want to see this. Why have I not seen this?" And I don't know if it's a product of New York City or just like, the world, where I'm like "I can't see everything, so I'm going to see nothing."

LF. It's super overwhelming.

SE. I think it was cool—not to plug Exponential—but I think—

LF. (We'll cut this part out.)

SE. Yeah, cut this: Exponential is so great because I think it does bring people from different performance-niche areas together for this centralized thing that you wouldn't necessarily—like if I was just in my little performance weirdo-bubble, I wouldn't necessarily always cross paths with certain people that I would like to cross paths with.

LF. I know, I mean, it's why these festivals are so tangibly important. And having heard your name, never having gone to your shows—it's simply a product of limited, finite time.

But also how does one—well—we get stuck, you know? You have your work, your shows, then once that's done you have to see your really close friends' shows or they'll be mad, and then after that, you have space for one more—

SE. Like Applebee's Time Square. What else are you gonna do with your time?

LF. I know! Anyway. I'm reading—or I read this book and then I am reading it again—it's called *Four Thousand Weeks*, which is—maybe you've heard of it.

SE. What is it?

LF. It's a little self-help-y. Or, like, at first you think it's a *little* self-help-y, but it's actually *insanely* self-help-y. It's so helped me—my—me self.

SE. *Four Thousand Weeks*?

LF. By Oliver Burkeman. And it's just about your—one's finitude on Earth. How time—how our concept of time—how we're doing ourselves so much damage by thinking we can control—anyway, that's my reason why I've never seen your work.

SE. "It's just, like, some British guy's fault." I know what you mean. One thing that struck me, I saw a lot of crossover in our work—through what I saw on Instagram and the videos you shared, and Helen Shaw's tweets about your show. I think one thing that super-resonated is how you don't take things too seriously. But you also take things very seriously. There's gravity to the work, but it's also—(*cuts throat*)

LF. Yeah.

SE. Your work was so cinematic, but also very silly. The humor is clear, but then it's also terrifying and beautiful and really strong, visually.

LF. Thank you. That's awesome.

SE. And I'm wondering, how do you wrestle with, I guess what I'll call "the darkness" and humor, and where do those little pockets come in for you?

LF. I feel like I always set out to make something honest, where it's like, "This time, I'm just gonna let whatever happens happen." But then I'm always charmed by observation. It's so much more interesting than what I have to offer. And I think some people make work from a deeply personal or experiential place. And I think I often make from an observational place. And that will often include darkness and humor pretty fast.

SE. Yeah.

LF. Because our world is so fucked and so jolly.

SE. Truly.

LF. It took me kind of a really long time to figure out that's what I was up to. In the last piece, in *Deepe Darknesse*, I had people being like, "Ah! The femininity!" And I was like, "Well, we were wearing dresses?"

SE. "There was lipstick?"

LF. Yeah, but because—there was obviously information from the world that was coming in, infusing the work, and then we were fucking with it and playing with it. And then you got this sort of seedy, like back-alley, sort of world. And then you just start to really want to live in the world because it's so fun. It's funny because one of your posts...I literally laughed so hard today reading your stuff. I laughed *so* hard. I couldn't stop. I was in the car, driving to a meeting, and I thought of the one where it's a gravestone, and it says something like, "Thanks, I am dead, but I'll get back to you as soon as possible."

> (*The post, an image of a tombstone, reads* "I HOPE THIS FINDS YOU WELL! I AM CURRENTLY DEAD BUT WILL GET BACK TO YOU AS SOON AS I CAN. MY BEST X")

I literally was dying. You use some imagery from *Harry Potter* and *The Lord of the Rings*, that ultra, ultra, ultra-mainstream pop culture stuff. And I think there's a lot of that swirling in my world too. But to answer your question, which I'm doing a bad job doing—

SE. No. You're doing it.

LF. I think it's about observing—trying to honestly observe the world, and through the act of observation, make a corridor, and then through that, you end up in a kind of twisted, dark, or sometimes light, sometimes funny, and sometimes serious reflection pool.

SE. That's awesome.

LF. It would be so nice to hear all about you. But we're doing each other. Which, since I've never seen your work, but seen markings of it on the internet (and also seeing the internet as a space where you're also producing work—which is really foreign to me and fascinating)—what is it about the liveness of performing?

SE. I feel like my origins are very much physical. And like, physical theater to dance—I was doing a lot of butoh-adjacent work for a long time and nothing was really online. And then when the pandemic hit, or the height of the pandemic hit, I didn't like performing on screens. I had a residency that was moved remotely and they were like "Perform on this square!"

LF. Horrid.

SE. And what was more fun were these memes that eventually became digital memes. And so I agreed to do a meme a day. So it's been going on three years of that. I find it more a tool for interfacing IRL. It's a lot of like, weird, niche faggoty things that are happening in my head that I then put out onto the internet. And it's kind of like a notebook.

LF. Sure.

SE. You know? So like, I can compile those ideas into performance, maybe?

LF. Yeah.

SE. But then there's always—a show I did at Exponential right before the pandemic hit was a fake M.F.A. show. And there were inklings of memes starting to happen.

LF. Yeah.

SE. And I feel like, for a long time, I was doing work that was very dark. And I was like, "I'm a dark dancer..." There was all this humor in it, but it was intense and people'd be like "That's hardcore!" And I'm like, "Great. I'm also very funny," and so I'd have to be like, writhing on the floor and be like, "Here's a joke about Celine Dion."

LF. Yeah.

SE. And then there's another part of me that was always just silly. And I'm like, "But I'm also really dark and have a lot of feelings and care about the world and I'm political!" And I feel like the internet space has helped me channel both of those things at the same time. Like the gravestone, that's a silly meme, but it's also like, "Oh fuck, that's real." And that's kind of where I live right now. I can't move as well as I used to—physical ailments have trickled in. And I'm still very embodied in my work, but it's just like finding that subtlety and that humor with less. And I feel like the internet—really honing in on like, a square image or a 30-second video—has taught me brevity in performance and how to be even more specific on top of the things that I've already done.

LF. It really does feel like a notebook. I didn't realize you were doing one a day.

SE. Yeah. Like one to three a day.

LF. Wow. I used to be such an avid notebook writer. Like, when you're young and you're like, "My ideas are so good! I must write them all down in My NoTeBoOk!" You know? And then you get older, and you're just like, "Well, one or two of them are good every few months." And then you remember them because there's so few. But anyway, I can really see how that would be such a useful tool. You're activating these ideas and then when you get into rehearsal rooms, they're recorded right there.

SE. And it was also something that just kept my creative practice alive. Like, "I *can't* leave my house. I *can* just fuck around on my laptop for 20 minutes before I sit down for the rest of the day."

LF. "Return to my sitting agenda."

SE. "Oh, I've got a busy day of sitting!" But yeah, it's cool to think about like, over my lifetime as a performing artist, where that creative energy goes. If it's a notebook, if it's memes, or if it's email drafts—I think it's important to record that kind of stuff.

LF. Are you in process for a show right now, for example?

SE. Yeah, I'm doing another show for Exponential 2024. It's called *ADMIN REVEAL*, which is about my memes.

LF. Was that—did you show some of that at a different—

SE. I did one last year, where I interviewed other meme artists who were also artists, like musicians or whatever, and let them share their work and then do a performance. And so it was more like facilitating, like interviewing. This will be more like interviewing myself.

LF. I was gonna say, if I were to walk into your rehearsal or to a showing of *ADMIN REVEAL*, what would I see?

SE. Um…just a lot of blood. None of it mine.

LF. Okay good.

SE. The work I make is always kind of low-tech—just pretty

bare bones. So this is mostly me in front of a screen. But also some performative elements. But yeah—I also like this idea that you brought forth about creating this play-space. I—especially when I was doing more butoh work—am always thinking about permission and accessibility, like, "How do I welcome people into the space? If I'm going to get dark, how do I create a space where people feel safe being in this?" Or safe being uncomfortable. And the same with humor: "How do you feel safe letting your guard down and laughing and being present?" And then, like you're saying, eventually you just create this world that you're happy to play in.

LF. Yeah.

SE. And I really like building that with an audience. Because then it becomes more fun to just fuck around together. I was reading one of your posts where you were thanking everyone about this last show. And you talked about how an audience is great and like, obviously a show shifts depending on the audience, but that your show is also the people who come to your fundraiser and the people who help you collaborate and every single person who touches the project, whether they're there for the final product or not. How do you conceptualize your performances with that in mind?

LF. It's just insane to me how hard it is—how hard it can be, how much help you need—how much of a team effort it is to make performance. Even the type of work I think we're probably both doing, which is deeply rooted in a DIY ethos—no one is making me do this. I mean, things are changing now. I do feel there's more pressure to produce "a thing" that is "the thing" and another "thing" that's connected to "that thing." But it's just a crazy thing to do. There are people who go above and beyond every single time. My community, my friends, my collaborators, my family, and my partner, everyone. And I'm like, "So they must believe in it too! They must feel something about this type of thing that we're doing, which is basically like, making an event for community to come to!" Like, it happens to be art, but ultimately, that's what it is—like, "They believe it's worth it?" And that is deeply moving. Because I think the type of thing that I've chosen—that works for me—is art as the anchor for time. And you know, a lot of people who had very deep artistic practices at some point sort of stopped ... and so, for whatever reason—because it's so fucking hard. The audience—they do *not* have to show up! And the fact that they do is never to be taken for granted, and I really cherish them. I really cherish the "showing up-ness" that it takes. When I feel like I'm not showing up, it really is painful. I'm just like, "I want to do that for everyone, too." It's my deepest joy. But you kind of have to sacrifice a little bit of that when you're making work. But yeah, it's definitely—as cheesy as it sounds—it takes a friggin village.

SE. It really does.

LF. Okay, so you have a show coming up in Exponential. I will be there. And I'm curious, because you mentioned you came from a dance background—or it's still part of your practice—and also butoh—dance is my background as well—I'm constantly grappling with dance as a form ... it always makes me ask why? And for what purpose? How do you think about dance? Is it important? Do you not care anymore? Is it just so deep in you that it's there, no matter how hard you try?

SE. It's important. Yeah, I feel like I do go through waves when I'm deeply in my Word Mind, where I'm just like, "I need to talk at you." And then times when I'm deeply in my body, where I'm like "I need to show you."

LF. Yes.

SE. And oftentimes I'm just kind of in the middle. And I found a lot of joy not labeling myself. I never called myself a capital D dancer. Because what does that mean? But I feel like dance does communicate something that words can't. And it can be a really powerful comedic tool. It can be a really powerful political tool. It can be a really powerful performative tool. So I do use it in a lot of work that I do. And finding those more distilled moments where I'm just like, "this feels good for movement."

LF. Yeah.

SE. Watching some of your clips of this last show—the very slow leg up—this distilled, really intentional movement— it's so powerful. When it's done well—which, I think you do it well—it's really impactful. And it also questions, like "What is dance?" If I'm just standing still and just moving something very slowly and intentionally...that's dance. Like I can do that sitting and talking about memes. But it's just time and place, I guess.

LF. Yeah, I agree. I battled it for so many years and have gone so far and returned. When I'm looking at your work online, I sense a similar sort of allegiance, almost like—for lack of a better word—the sort of stubborn belief that there is something to it. I struggle with a lot of the dance world. I get bored a lot. I want more. I want to see stuff happening. Give me something to look at. And because the body is the most interesting of all tools, I'm easily frustrated. I like maximalism—I like things that are in your face. But I think dance is a truth machine. You can do whatever you want. But if you're moving, that's *you*. And that's, like, terrifying for me, because I don't think that my work is autobiographical or diaristic or whatever, but when you start moving—

SE. You're saying something.

LF. Yeah, and I love—that's why I will always cherish being a dancer, as much as I'm like "I'm actually an experimental theater-maker and I make like *embodied* work but it's sort of like anti-disciplinary or—" (LISA *pantomimes vomiting*). Sometimes I'm like, "I'm a dancer and I make dance." And then you come see the show and it's like, "Where was the dance? I'm not totally sure."

SE. Yeah, genre is stupid.

LF. So stupid. And yet, almost on the daily, you gotta come up with something.

SE. Yeah, it's like what is this label for? Who is this label for? "Why don't *you* just tell me? What do *you* think you just saw?"

EVAN SILVER + CHRISTINA TANG

EVAN SILVER *first presented their work,* cryptochrome, *in the 2023 Exponential Festival. Silver often performs in character as the oracle Tiresias.*

CHRISTINA TANG *first presented her work,* TRAFFIC, *with Exponential in 2022, returning in 2024 with* DIRT *under the auspices of her theater company, Sour Milk, and featuring collaborators from* TRAFFIC. *Christina first worked with Exponential in 2018 as a lighting designer on Brett Evan Solomon and Kelsey Lurie's* SOMEONEPLEASELISTENANDUNDERSTAND(they're wiretapping our brains).

CHRISTINA TANG. I was watching the video of *cryptochrome*, and I was very engaged with your figure and how you looked and how extreme it was. And then also how structural that room and that performance by the dancer was. And I was wondering, like, what was that relationship like for you?

EVAN SILVER. Between my body and the space?

CT. Yeah, and your aesthetic being very severe, I think, and then how natural the performer was.

ES. I think it was important for me to feel like audiences could engage with the material in a variety of ways. And so one way is to close your eyes and lie down and dream. One is to watch (*dancer*) Mizuho Kappa engaging in the space in this more fluid, organic way. And one is to watch me. And

I think this expression that might feel harsh or severe is also a stripping down of this persona that is often much more extravagant, and over the top, and audacious. I actually just wore the things that I felt really comfortable in. And I felt like this sort of bat-like creature that could disappear into the shadows or something.

CT. Well, maybe the video is just like, specific. Like, you're kind of far away and the performer is closer. And then there are moments where I'm drawn to you and you are my focus and you are the creature (cryptochrome *consists of vignettes of poetry concerning different animals and "creatures"*). And then I was always more aware of how these natural things that you were describing came across. And I thought it worked very well because I—instead of just hearing you say (*paraphrasing text from* cryptochrome) "You are a little mole, you are soft and fuzzy," I was like you, Evan, could be one too. If that makes sense.

ES. How do you engage with the idea of the "natural" in your work? You're dealing with all these new technologies, new media, this hybrid-video-game theater form. Is the question of the natural something that you think about? Or the natural versus the artificial? Or is there a different set of parameters that you're looking at?

CT. I'd say probably a different set of parameters. I don't want to say I don't think about it all the time, but I think I'd probably categorize it more like: what do people expect and why do they expect it? I am a person who is not very fond of being on stage and I don't really like personally engaging with embodiment, which is why we were talking earlier about you being a performer, and that freaking me out a lot as a practice. But I think my question for you is about why that representation. Most of my practice is about, "Why this representation? And who does it? And how does that serve the storytelling?"

ES. I'm also realizing maybe there's an answer to your question that is more obvious: probably the thing that makes it read most unnatural is my painted face with the gash through it.

CT. Mm-hmm.

ES. And, for me, this white circle that I typically wear as Tiresias is really a reference to the mask. I have found that through the form of this persona, through the form of Tiresias, I can actually excavate or liberate or expose these parts of myself that can't find form through Evan, right, this sort of "natural" human form. And that by creating this persona that allows for these cyborg, hybrid, multi-species possibilities, I can actually become something that maybe even feels truer to me, even if it is less "natural," right? I'm not wearing what we call a "natural" face, right, a kind of "natural" beauty—we don't think of a clown face, you know. But I think artifice—and I feel this really broadly in the arts, and not just in my own practice—I feel that artifice is the pathway to excavating the thing that exists beneath the surface, right? The illusion of Realism, or of Naturalism is that reality is skin deep. And for me, it's actually something much deeper and more ineffable, and harder to describe than that. And sometimes by creating things that are highly artificial, highly manufactured, technological, maybe "unnatural," we can access the thing that is underneath the surface.

CT. This is something I talk a lot about. How do you know

what is real to you? My specific gripe with theater these days is I feel like it's really kind of pigeonholed itself, because it's saying like, "What is real?" and, "What is theater?" And like, as a definition, theater is live and it is now. And therefore it can't keep up with film, it can't keep up with TV, because it can't be all those things all at the same time.

ES. Yeah.

CT. And in the past, we would call TV "teleplays." And theater was real. So there's just a televised version of a play. But now we're doing theater that's replicating what's online, because that's the movement of what's real. And I think—I really love your answer about it being abstract, and you can get something a little bit more real, because I feel like in the future it's going to be somewhere in between. Like, we aren't going to only define our lives by how I see you here and now. There are going to be other aspects of us that exist in spaces that feel just as real because that is just how technology is going to be moving us. I love this idea that you can be more of who you are with these other aspects excavated, like you said. And to not be stuck with how we physically are or come across in a single-faceted way. I've had these conversations with my collaborators as well. And one of the conversations we had was this is what kind of makes digital spaces very naturally queer.

ES. Mmm...

CT. Because you don't have to be tied to the one presentation.

ES. There's a scholar who writes about mediatization in theater. And there's this pretty accepted dogma that you're referring to that theater is the thing that disappears, theater is defined by liveness and presence. And I think I still buy into a lot of that. But the argument that this scholar is making is that actually, now we really live in a time where the sort of "purity" of that model no longer exists. Things are recorded and processed—the moment you incorporate any kind of video or projection technology, the moment something is filmed on a phone...Like, certainly, if you're exploring some kind of hybrid-video-game form, you're also challenging this way of thinking about theater as something that is a kind of pure liveness, right?

CT. That's true.

ES. Do you feel like liveness operates in your work in a different way than maybe in a more traditional theatrical context? Or, how are you interested in playing with this idea of liveness?

CT. That is—that is my thing. I think we're probably referencing the same book. And I also similarly cannot remember who wrote it.

ES. Do you (*indicating* NIC) remember?

NIC ADAMS. No.

CT. It's called like, it's called *Liveness*.

ES. Yeah, it's called *Liveness*. I think I feel like his last name starts with an A. Philip Auslander.

CT. Yes!

ES. Okay, great.

CT. Yeah, I read that when I was in college, I was like, "This is blowing my mind." Because I had been a really nervous

31

kid. And I was always online and I didn't know what to do with myself in real life. And it felt like I was a better version of myself online. It took a very long time to be, like, cool with me *here*. And also be the same person here as I am online. And maybe they're different—to exist in both those kinds of spaces. And I always think about that when I make theater. And so my thing that I try to do in my practice, that I'm only just starting to develop, is how do you do digital *live*? Like if you're presenting live and it says, like, "Here and now, same time, same place," is that the same when you're online? Because what online lets you do is extract and make things asynchronous. You can do things that affect the same place, but not at the same time. You can do things that are at the same time that have nothing to do with each other. Can you even be in the same place online? And I have no answers whatsoever. But I am very curious what that's going to look like in the future. How do we continue that conversation on both sides? Like how we pull in elements of a different format, different ways of communicating in digital spaces, or in live spaces, and blending those into more hybrid connections. And to me, the things that were always best at that were video games because you get to be online, hang out, and feel like you're in a real place.

ES. Mmm...

CT. But, you know, that's a very specific thing. And not an open toolbox for many people. So, again, I have no answers, but I'm trying to find ways to access those things and use them for projects.

ES. How do you engage with interactivity? Especially in the

context of thinking about participatory theater versus the video game, how are those things similar? How are they different?

CT. I talk about this a lot with the people I work with, Anna Jastrzembski and Carsen Joenk, and the conclusion that we came to was that people have to feel like the decisions they make mean something. And that's, again, very broad, but it's very easy to get caught in the narrative of "Oh, well they get to push a button and therefore it's interactive." Like, that's not it. Or I guess that is interactive, but is it meaningful? If it feels like the people are what's pushing that story along, or that something they decided on changed something tangibly—you might vote for something, but it's like, if the choice you make doesn't matter, or you get railroaded into a decision and if you're upset about it even... what was the whole point?

ES. It was cheap.

CT. Because there's always those cheap tricks and sometimes the cheap tricks work, because people get to do something with their hands. And that keeps them engaged. So that's another level of design and direction. You get another sensory experience that—you get to physically do something. I forgot the thread of that question.

ES. Now I'm also following other threads, like this idea of tactility. And the video game is also really interesting to me, doing something with your hands. Often, I imagine somebody playing a video game, you know, doing the thing with their hands...but I think that's different than the kinds of tactility you're talking about in a theatrical context.

CT. Yeah.

ES. That's just very interesting. I'm wondering how you engage with these different kinds of embodiment, right?

CT. Yeah.

ES. Like, in your work. It sounds more like the audience is part of the video game, rather than an embodied form that is displacing themselves into this video form.

CT. Exactly. I've been saying to people, "audience-driven conflict" and "audience-generated conflict," but it's that idea that the audience is what's making the content happen. We are providing the structure, and that's the endless—the piece I did for Exponential in 2022 was called *TRAFFIC*. And we had like 60 toy cars that were part of this game system that you could see on a live stream, and people could, using their phones, choose which car to be, and then make decisions for the cars, and puppeteer-performers would move them. And then, because of the decisions that people made, conflict was created by—performed by—the audience, and the performers got to make that happen. And it felt like people were into it, because they're like, "Oh, well, I pushed a button on my thing. And something happened on screen and a person's hand is holding it."

ES. Yeah.

CT. It's that simple. But how do we take that another step further? I'm always like, "Well, we can guide them to a certain extent, it's always going to be narrative in a certain way, but it's going to be nonlinear...we have to define the narrative, or else it's just not interesting." People don't want to engage in total chaos, they want to feel guided. So how do we create a format that's about the interaction, but like, still leads to something that gets to convey a narrative—maybe a more open-ended narrative. But it will always have the perspective of me and Carsen and Anna because we're the people writing it or developing it.

NA. I wonder if there's a throughline with performing in clubs and interactivity. Like, Evan, you perform works on stage and in nightlife. How do you think about the audience and their differences in those two spaces?

ES. You know, what we've been talking about raises a set of questions for me about where agency is located in the production of creative work and, maybe on one extreme, there's the auteur director who decides every little thing and the actors are pawns and the audience sits and folds their arms. And then at the other extreme, there's, I don't know, the pure chaos of…a park. Just people existing. No one's in control. We're all riding the reality together. Which is maybe not art?

CT. Maybe it is.

ES. Maybe it is. I'm finding there's something really exciting and generative about these middle spaces where the audience is really participating in the creation of the work. And so this flying moment, for example, that happened last night, I got to be this giant, weird puppet-god flying on a zipline across the House of Yes. I teched it on Friday. I teched it last night before the doors opened, but the performance—the work itself—was a collaboration with a crazy audience of people screaming and dancing and reaching up and trying to touch me.

CT. Yeah.

ES. And the only relationship that that performance bears to the tech is literally the technicality of what's happening. The safety procedure, you know? But that was absolutely an immersive, interactive, participatory work happening in real time that I couldn't really foresee until I was engaging directly with the audience in the creation of that moment... which was very fun.

CT. Yeah, they always say like, the audience is the last element of a theater performance. How do you want audiences to engage with your work?

ES. I think it depends on the work, it depends on the project. I would say, coming from a theater background, I am more comfortable with the version where you create a piece, and then the audience receives it. That feels safer and more comfortable. But that doesn't mean that's what I should be doing. And it's actually very exciting, especially in this kind of hybrid performance that's at the intersection of theater and nightlife, for there to be parts of a work that are contingent and responsive and reactive to what's happening in the space and what's happening in the audience. And you can feel the way that people connect to you and hook into the work. When they can tell you're listening to them. And they can tell you're with them. Like—it's a very small detail— but I brought this show *UNDERWORLD* to Berlin in August, and it was mycelium-themed. And we, for *UNDER-WORLD*—which is specifically designed for nightclubs, and is a combination of scripted and unscripted—there was a moment where I'm introducing this live mushroom as this weird organism from another kingdom—

CT. Did you bring the mushrooms?

ES. Yes, yes. A whole thing of oyster mushrooms, planted in a mannequin.

CT. Oh my god.

ES. And I was like "Pleurotus has"—this is the scientific term for oyster mushrooms—"has no legs, no arms, no heart, no brain." And someone in the audience was like, "Sexy." And I was like, "Sexy! That's *right*." And then we had this moment where everyone just got into the sexiness of the mushroom. And it was partly because people were so excited that there was this responsivity, that we were making something—this new affect in the space about the mushroom.

CT. That's interactive.

ES. That's interactive, yeah.

CT. I love that you brought a mushroom. It's so camp, in a way. Also, I would want to touch it and to meet the mushroom.

ES. Yeah.

CT. When you do this performance—can I see this mushroom?

ES. That one I think is non-transferable.

CT. Do you have photos?

ES. Yeah.

CT. Afterwards, I want to see.

ES. And I want to see your cars. Are they puppet cars?

CT. They're just Matchbox cars. They're just batches of like shitty collectibles that nobody wanted off eBay.

ES. Okay, so maybe we should find a way to close on like, what we love about puppetry. Why is that such an interesting form to us?

CT. You go first.

ES. Oh god. I think there is something about the displacement of life and agency into these other forms that are non-human that maybe allows us to cultivate different kinds of empathy, different kinds of understanding, different kinds of perception. I think I'm also really attracted to animist philosophies and ideas that there's a kind of life or consciousness imbued in matter—and that there's a way of activating that through puppetry that can be unsettling and disturbing, but also dislodges our solid understandings about reality. And that feels generative as an artist, right? What about you?

CT. I think it's similar. I feel like there are possibilities in objects that we as humans can't conceive of, and that it allows us to not be tied to Naturalism and Realism that—if we see it, we get to understand it a bit better. We are so non-abstract. It's hard to bring audiences to abstraction. But puppets, because they're usually an exciting object that we want to believe in, they're...we believe in them in a way that we couldn't believe if we saw a human do it. It lets us, like you said, empathize. And if it's charismatic, you get to put your own little hope and faith into it as a character in a way that you wouldn't necessarily, like—with another person, you might be combative with them. You're not really going to combat a puppet. I think.

ES. That part.

TRISTAN ALLEN + DAVID GREENSPAN

*DAVID GREENSPAN starred in the 2023 Expo-
nential Festival production of Joey Merlo's*
On Set with Theda Bara. *Greenspan is a
playwright and performer and the recipient
of numerous awards, including six OBIES.
Also in 2023, Exponential presented* TRISTAN
ALLEN'S Tin Iso and the Dawn. *Both productions took place at The Brick Theater in
Williamsburg, just a couple of weeks apart.*

*This conversation, as well as the three that
follow, took place in front of a live audience
at Brick Aux in October 2023.*

DAVID GREENSPAN. You told me something interesting while
we were waiting earlier about your great-grandfather, who
was an artist. Can you tell people about that?

TRISTAN ALLEN. Yeah. His name was Marc Moutillet. He
fought for the French in World War II. My family tells me
he fought without a bullet in his gun. And he was taken
into war camps, and escaped with a group of gypsies south,
and then ended up becoming a surrealist painter. And my
name is Tristan Marc Moutillet Allen. So I'm named after
him. And he has a lot of paintings in the house I grew up
in. And a lot of them are of my naked mother. Yeah.

DG. Did the work that you saw—or other parts of your family
life—encourage you in terms of becoming an artist, or lead
you towards work in the arts? Do those paintings have

anything to do with your development in terms of artistic interests?

TA. Yeah, absolutely. There was no choice. My mom was a dancer, and my dad did a lot of scenic design.

DG. Oh wow.

TA. I'm very happy there wasn't a choice, you know? It just kind of ...was very lucky to grow up around things like what they were doing.

DG. So you grew up in New York or somewhere else?

TA. Yeah, I grew up in a village called Saratoga Springs.

DG. Oh right, you mentioned that.

TA. I kind of bounced between Saratoga and Quebec, which is where all my family was. I have a question for you. So you did *On Set with Theda Bara* at The Exponential Festival this past January. As a one-person show, how much influence did you have over the writing by Joey Merlo and direction by Jack Serio? And how did the initial ideas come about? And—this is a two-parter—what are you good at? What are you bad at? And how do you know what to delegate?

DG. In terms of Joey's play, I did a reading for Joey, a reading of another play of his when he was still at Brooklyn College. And we got on, and then he had written this play, *On Set with Theda Bara*, with—for those of you who don't know, Theda Bara was a silent movie star. There's very little of Bara left because all the film wasn't really kept in those days. She was known as the the original vamp. Her Cleopatra, there's literally 10 seconds left. So he wrote this play about her and some other characters. And we did a reading of it. It was much—it was rather long. And then they got into The Exponential Festival. And Joey and his director, Jack Serio, called me and said, "Can you be in this play?" And I said, "Sure." So we did it. And we did get together beforehand. About two weeks before I needed to start rehearsal they had a script, we went over it, and I did share some thoughts about it. So there was a little bit of input.

TA. Sure.

DG. But I do feel very strongly—I would suspect all artists feel this way—that when you're a creative artist, a generative artist, *you* have the final say in what stays and what goes, and I always try to respect that because I work with a lot of playwrights as an actor. So I had some input.

TA. Sure.

DG. What was the second part?

TA. Just like ...you work with other people. Still, it's you alone up there. But what do you feel like you need other people for, in order to be up there in the first place? Like what *can't* you do?

DG. Well, you need a play. Sometimes I act in my own plays, but either way, you need a play. So someone has to write it. And it's good to have a director most of the time because you need someone to look at it and see what is working and what might *not* be working. I mean, I iron my own clothes, and I'll do whatever I have to do to get on stage.

TA. Just another question about that show. She said, "The reason good women like me and flock to my pictures is that there's a little bit of vampire instinct in every woman." Do you relate to that? Do you feel like you've found your vampire instinct in this production?

DG. Well, I think when she was talking about vamp, I think it had to do with a level of seduction. It wasn't so much—well maybe it was predatory to some extent. It was a lot about seduction, it was a lot about control. And I suppose every person has a sense of sensual control or a desire for this kind of sensual control. You're wondering if I found it?

TA. I mean—

DG. At my age?

(*Laughter.*)

TA. It's supposed to be in every woman, you know?

DG. Right…I would think it'd be in every person, though.

TA. Yeah.

DG. And what came first, the music or the puppetry?

TA. The music.

DG. The music.

TA. I studied piano and have been making music since I was really little. And then I kind of fell in love with music that maybe isn't the best to see performed, you know? Electronic music, things like that…where you would much rather close your eyes. And the kind of work I do—I'm trying to tell a story without words. And my music is instrumental. I needed some sort of accompaniment that would allow me to tell my story without dictating it. And I don't believe that anybody chooses puppetry, I think it just happens to people.

DG. Really? What do you mean by that?

TA. Well, I mean, it happened to me for sure.

DG. How did it happen?

TA. And a lot of freaks running around, they say the same thing.

DG. Well, how did it happen?

TA. When I moved to New York, I had two and a half months to find work. And I auditioned at a marionette children's theater called Puppetworks in Park Slope. I ended up working there doing two to three puppet shows a day, five days a week, for almost three years. And it just really became my life. Before that, I was always interested in puppetry. I saw my first puppet shows in Bali. And I really like wayang kulit, which is the shadow puppetry that goes along with gamelan which is traditional multimedia stuff in Bali. And my dad, at the beginnings of Bread and Puppet Theater, I mean, he worked with them, and he had a paper-mâché blue angel that he would put on the top of our Christmas tree that was from the Bread and Puppet. And there were these dusty suitcases in the basement that had an assortment of different puppets down there that I thought were really cool. So it was, like, under the surface. And I plan to continue to make music and perform the music with puppetry for as long as I can.

DG. Groovy.

TA. I watched *Theda Bara*. It's incredible. It's a lot of talking.

What about being on stage allows you to communicate things that you wouldn't in everyday life?

DG. Well, it varies on what you're acting in. If you're acting in a play in a more conventional sense, where you're playing opposite other actors—if it's a linear or narrative play, you're just engaged in conversation or in actions. If it's not a conventional kind of script, if it was Gertrude Stein or something, then there's another range of expression. In a solo play where there's both speaking to the audience, as well as conversations between the characters, it's partly the matter of inviting people into the story with you and, you know, breaking that fourth wall and telling them a story. Or showing them how to listen to a story. I've done solo renditions of conventional plays—I did this solo rendition of *Strange Interlude* by Eugene O'Neill, which is a six-hour play. I played eight characters, and they had inner monologues as well as internal asides. So in that sense, I was never talking to the audience. It was only conversations through the characters, and also their internal thoughts. So in that sense, it was simply playing scenes, it was acting. When you're doing a play where you talk to the audience, there is a different relationship established. But I'm very careful to still leave a boundary up. For me, as an actor, at least, I like to put an audience at ease, in the sense that nothing is expected of the audience. I'm there to engage them, I'm there to entertain them. I'm there to give them an experience. And I want them to feel perfectly safe. That's important in a setting where you're talking to them—and often very close to them—that even though there *seems* to be a performative relationship that's not conventional, they're still—I'm doing the performing. Does that make sense?

TA. Yeah, that makes sense. Absolutely.

DG. Do you still like classical music? Did you study classical music?

TA. I studied jazz. Yeah. I mean, I like all sorts of music. My heart's not in it at all.

DG. In what?

TA. In classical or jazz.

DG. It's so funny because I was telling my partner who's knowledgeable about classical music—he listened to your music and he responded to it really, in a sense—he listened to the Chopin preludes—and it reminded him of that kind of material. It's so odd that you say you don't have an interest in classical music.

TA. I do. I like it a lot. But…yeah, that's not really…no, just to answer your question. No, I don't.

DG. And what about jazz? Would you still listen to more—did you grow up with traditional jazz or…?

TA. Yeah, I mean, I learned some Chopin. I learned Satie and Ravel and Debussy, and I really liked the Expressionist pianists, the ones that are very muddy and keep the pedal down and everything kind of washes over you …I really love that style. With jazz there's also—there's this expected room to kind of go where you want to go with any given idea. And I actually felt that the academics behind jazz were kind of more confining than classical. At least—everything had to shift at such a fast pace that I always felt like I was kind of running up a hill, catching my breath. Especially when it comes to working with other ensemble musicians. I think I learned in studying music, that I didn't want to be a musician. I was around a lot of athletes and people that were very, very good at the craft. And I was not. I'm very happy I had that experience because it gave me a set of years to really be like, "Oh, I'm not going to be a pianist. I'm gonna use piano and make things, but I don't want to be a pianist." And I would have spent my whole life having to figure that out.

DG. Do you use improvisation?

TA. Yes, I have a skeleton and then I kind of flesh it out. Would you say you're primarily an actor?

DG. No. I consider myself as much a playwright as an actor, except I appear in my own plays; whenever I write a play, I appear in it. So I consider myself a thespian.

TA. Thespian's a good one.

DG. I'm engaged in the theater.

SLETH + CAMERON STUART

CAMERON STUART *first presented his play,* GERMANY 1933, *in the 2017 Exponential Festival with his theater company, Saints of an Unnamed Country. Performances took place at The Glove, a venue Stuart founded with friends and which partnered with Exponential until its closure in 2019. Stuart would go on to present* Police in the Wilderness *at the 2020 festival. In addition to his work as a playwright, director, and venue partner, Stuart was also a member of the Exponential curatorial and administrative team for many years.*

In 2018, SLETH *co-wrote and performed in* THE SPOOKY CLASSROOM FOR EXPERIMENTAL ETHICS *at The Glove. Co-written with Forest Entsminger, the duo would return for the 2019 festival with* Sexless Cocaine Saturday, *co-created with Scott Ries.*

CAMERON STUART. So...you know, my mom's a Gemini. What's it like to be a Gemini?

SLETH. I have a great time. Life is pretty nice. You know, the reason that I'm Sleth now—I used to be Seth—is that I had the more fun side of myself, which became Sleth, and then Seth went away. So that's partially, I think, Gemini.

CS. Nice.

SL. Yeah. I remember the first time that I met you, and I think we've gone on kind of separate trajectories, yet come back and forth—but I saw you at The Glove when I was performing *The Spooky Classroom for Experimental Ethics*. And you were running around, you were getting everything ready, and you were the most wonderful host for us. I would love to hear a little bit about The Glove and your time running that space.

CS. You know, the funny thing that we always say about The Glove is that we can't remember any of it—

SL. Sure.

CS.—which is both partially true and a way to weasel out of it. But I will say that my friends and I were living at this place called the Bohemian Grove, which was pretty low on the rung of DIY spaces in Bushwick. Other people had better sound systems or cooler-looking spaces, but ours was literally a basement. When we started, the floor was unfinished, and there were all these rickety lights, and sometimes it would flood with toilet water. But then we became kind of the last people surviving because, you know, Bushwick started to get developed and suddenly everybody was like, "Oh, can we get a show at the Bohemian Grove?" And we were like, "Ah, it's our time to shine!" And then ...we got shut down by our landlord. So then we thought, well, "Maybe we should keep this party going." So we found a warehouse not too far away, we cobbled enough money together—it was exactly the right deal for us—and rented it out. And just, you know, we had the experience of running these basement shows and so we translated that into the warehouse. And we were very open to the people who came. And we were kind of like, "This is how we know how to do things but tell us—you know—what you're thinking and then we'll meet you in the middle." And that's pretty much how we ran it for three years.

SL. And you had like many, many, many shows there.

CS. Oh, yeah. The bread and butter was noise music or art rock bands or art rock noise bands. But we fit in a lot of other stuff, you know, ranging from comedy, these crazy variety nights, which we called Weirdwick, named by—he probably doesn't remember this—Ryan Downey came up with that name. We had a couple of other theater things. We had dance, performance art, fashion shows ... at one point yoga, which didn't really make any sense—

SL. You got to do something during the daytime.

CS. So I remember when you came to do *The Spooky Classroom for Experimental Ethics*, you were part of Flux Factory.

SL. I was.

CS. Are you still with Flux Factory?

SL. Oh, yeah.

CS. Oh cool. Well, how did you get involved with Flux?

SL. I was a little idiot down in Texas. I was in San Antonio. I was living on this farm run by Alison Ward and Shane Heinemeier, who are two longtime Flux Factory people. Alison is a performance artist. For a long time, she's been like my performance mother, but I was living with them on the farm, and they're like, "You should apply to this residency." And I did and it was a wild time for a child from San Antonio to live with, like 20 international artists, and it was a really great time for me. It's where Forest and

49

I really started. Forest Entsminger is my main collaborator. If you know them, they made The Brick accessible, like handicap accessible, and they fixed the bathroom. They can do everything. They're the best. So—

cs. And you know Forest from Texas.

sl. We know each other from Texas. We met when we were 17.

cs. And so I was getting ready for this talk tonight and I was looking through all these links that Nic handily made available to us, and I started playing this video, *Hand Stuff*—

sl. *Hand Stuff*.

cs. And my partner, Stephanie, from across the room is like, "What is that?? I love that!! I want to know more about it." So where was that? Was that at House of Yes?

sl. It was at House of Yes, which is the main people that produce my work right now. I'm often in their circus variety shows. *Hand Stuff* is one of my favorite new pieces. It started—from like 2018 to 2020 I did a comedic fisting act, which was very wonderful and really brought a lot of joy to my life and a lot of range to my performance career. And it was with a delightful friend named Punch Boy, and I was named Makita Spin after the drill brand, and we would just, you know, do these comedic numbers where I was inside of him the whole time and we lip-synced and we danced. We had little costumes, did little stories, and *Hand Stuff* is one of my main pieces now.

cs. So in this video, you enter upside down on this crucifix.

sl. Yeah.

CS. Is Forest involved in this at all?

SL. No, Forest is currently the star of their scenic design program at Yale. So I've really been focusing on my solo performance work, and House of Yes just like affords these insane opportunities to me. So I come in, suspended from a cross, upside down, in my manic clown makeup, and I deliver this monologue about fisting God and discovering what accidental Love from God feels like for a queer person, because it's not something we're expected to feel.

CS. Yeah, I love the writing, and, you know, that was something that I saw kind of connected all your pieces in Exponential. You had *Sexless Cocaine Saturday*, which was at The Brick, and then *THE SPOOKY CLASSROOM FOR EXPERIMENTAL ETHICS*, and in both of them the language and the writing were so great. And there was also this very madcap, but also satirical vibe. So it was, you know, not too conceptual, but there was this conceptual throughline ... What's your background? Did you start writing and then start performing? Were you performing and then writing, or was it a simultaneous Gemini birth?

SL. I studied directing for theater and quickly got into experimental—like, theater that I made with this group of seven people in San Antonio. And we were just constantly making shows and like, rehearsing all night, and then working, like, bakery jobs and back-of-house things. I always took the director role, but then, probably six or seven years ago, started writing and really enjoyed that. Forest and I would write everything together. *Sexless Cocaine Saturday* we wrote with Scott Ries. We went to P-town together and watched *Face/Off*, which is an incredible film and that was the inspiration for the whole thing. I'd love to hear more about your theater company. And the name is escaping me right now.

CS. That's because I changed it.

SL. You changed it.

CS. I remember this conversation with Sanaz, another of our panelists. We were at an Exponential Festival admin meeting one day, talking about how, on a whim, you name a theater company. And then seven years later—

SL. It's on your resume forever.

CS. "I thought that was just for that one event!" So I moved to New York and my idea was, I was going to become this playwright. And I had this friend down South named Shitty Bedford, and—

SL. Wait. Please say his name—

CS. His name is—

SL. We love—

CS. His name is Shitty Bedford, and he lives now in the western part of Georgia in a house that he built himself. Anyway, so I moved up here, and we had been doing some theater down South in Atlanta when we were both living there, and he was like, "Oh, good job, Bob. You know"—he calls me Bob—he said, "Good job, Bob. Good job moving up to New York, you know? I hear you're doing well, you getting all these plays produced. But you know you should have me come up there and we should do a play together." And I was like, "Okay, yeah, sure. Why not?" So then, you know, the next day I was out and I was like, "This looks like a pretty cool space. What's this? Secret Project Robot? Can I do a show here?" And they're like, "Sure." Apparently, this is not normal. People don't get to do shows at Secret Project Robot. But I was just like, "Cool! I guess my theater company's named ...Saints of an Unnamed Country" and then that was the beginning. Yeah, it was that silly. And then the next day, I was calling people on the phone being like, "Who wants to be in my show? Shitty Bedford is coming to town!"

SL. When was the Shitty Bedford show?

CS. That was in 2012. And Shitty Bedford has his own theater company—I will plug him because he's a wonderful, wonderful human—named Hot Shit! Theater Company.

SL. Hot shit...

CS. The last show I was in that he did was called *Oh Fearsome Head, Part III*. And I played the Bugman.

SL. The Bugman. Yes. Where is he? Where is Shitty Bedford?

CS. He owns his own land which he calls Waxon Gibbons. But he also bought his neighbor's land, which is called Palookaville. So together they're the Sacred Territory, so technically he now lives on the Sacred Territories full time.

SL. And in this collaboration, did you do the writing? Shitty did the writing? Both?

CS. He writes for his own theater company.

SL. Okay.

cs. But he's also quite a handy designer and he works very often for this theater company down in Atlanta called Dad's Garage. It's a pretty popular improv theater company that has been around in Atlanta for a long time. So anyway, he's very handy. He can build anything. And his design is wild. So he would come in and do design work on my shows. So for the first show, he made these big wooden animal masks that looked wonderful, but they were miserable to wear. I have this giant one that made me look like a wolf.

sl. Did the Bugman have a mask?

cs. No, but halfway through one of my songs I turned into this character named Xaxax. And I magically pull this sword out of a pistol or something. And then they would encase me in this wooden-like skirt. And then I elevated and this entire band played "Oh Fearsome Head, Part III," and I started singing it. I don't know what it meant but it was amazing.

sl. That's great.

cs. Yeah, so back to the Sleth-verse. When you were at The Glove you were on a split bill.

sl. Yeah.

cs. And that was a really fun experience for me to have, you know, all these different artists coming through. I was kind of interested in what your experience was. That was the first time you were in the festival. What did you think of the whole thing?

sl. It was really quite an experience for us because we had done *The Spooky Classroom for Experimental Ethics* as an installation. Like we were in The Wassaic Project's haunted house, and it'd be like a lot of children coming in, and we would like corrupt their sense of what ethics was. And teach them how easy it is to be corrupted. So then we got to do it as an actual theater piece, and have like a captive audience for 30 minutes, instead of our 10-minute children audience. And that was really phenomenal. We got to expand the piece, we got to expand these two characters. Forest and I played these, like, very questionable scientist-wives, who were interested in seeing what they could get away with. We had these really beautiful projections that Forest drew that were all black and white, and they really fit in so well with the space and it made this kind of like, full nightmare in the round. It was very fun.

cs. I remember there was a survey too, right?

sl. There was a survey and it ended with asking everyone to draw their favorite childhood pet as a way to get them really involved. And then we would shred it in front of them. Which was super fun. So mean. We gave them 10 minutes to draw. Yeah, it was remarkable. We got to see a lot of crazy stuff that year. You know, I saw Bailey Williams' *Buffalo Bailey's Ranch for Gay Horses, Troubled Teen Girls and Other* in Exponential and it changed my life. Because I saw it and thought, "This is a perfect play." I Facebook-friended Bailey and then eventually we became roommates. And my life changed. But yeah, Exponential is always just a great time to see weird shit. What's something that you've never done onstage you'd like to do?

cs. I think I've done everything—

sl. Yeah, but the one thing.

cs. Retire.

sl. Great. Sick.

cs. No, I guess I mean—I'm one of these people that just cannot get enough of performing. And yet, I seemingly spend my days sitting about, thinking to myself, "I just cannot wait until I never have to perform again!" And then it'll be like, (*telephone rings*) "Hello? Yes, of course I'm free to perform on that date." And then I'll dash to my closet and be like, "Ah ha! This is the dress! I've been waiting for this moment!" Before long, I'm racing about town, spending gobs of money on all the necessary accessories. And then after it's all over and the performance is done, I'll suddenly revert to: "No, I will never do that again. No! That was the last time! I swear." So yeah, it's impossible to know what I want to do until that phone rings. How about you?

sl. Like you, I've done a lot. I've put my hands in a lot of things onstage. And I would really love an audience to just go to town throwing tomatoes at me. Audiences aren't afforded that anymore, like if they don't like something they don't get to throw tomatoes. I would love to give that to people.

BEN HOLBROOK + SANAZ B TENNENT

SANAZ B TENNENT *presented her play,* TALK BACK, *in the 2019 Exponential Festival and shot and directed a short film called* ENTER PORTER, *with text by Jess Almasy, for the 2021 festival. She directed Elinor T. Vanderburg's* BLOODSHOT *in the 2020 festival, as well as a short film entitled* BLOODSHOT: The Call *in 2021, both of which featured* BEN HOLBROOK *as an actor. Sanaz has also served as a curator for the festival, in addition to writing the newsletters in 2021 and 2024.*

In addition to his acting work in various Exponential productions, including those aforementioned and Allyson Dwyer's Arrow of Time *in 2023, Ben wrote, directed, performed, and produced a theatrical guided meditation entitled* Theater Immaterial *for Exponential in 2021.*

SANAZ B TENNENT. Let's say we're on a date.

BEN HOLBROOK. Okay.

ST. Where would you take me?

BH. Oh, wow. Um, jeez. I was not prepared. I don't know. Maybe—

ST. Like, would it be indoors? Outdoors?

BH. I think partially, I think it'd be like a two-part thing.

ST. Okay.

BH. So maybe like some sort of like, garden or park or something, maybe for a picnic. And then, like a show or museum afterward?

ST. What if it rains?

BH. Depends on how you feel about being out in the rain.

ST. I'm into it. Yeah.

BH. Oh, great. Okay. The plans don't change.

ST. Okay, so now I hear that you write poetry and also plays and you also make films and other things. We'll get to that. But actually, my question was, if you were going to write me a poem—

BH. Mmhmm.

ST. What would be the title? And would it include the word love?

BH. I asked you a question a second ago. And I'm trying to remember what your response was. I think it was "Okay, um..."

ST. Okay, um?

BH. "Okay, um."

ST. That's the name of the poem?

BH. I think—that's the name of the poem. Yeah.

ST. And you've won a lot of awards...?

BH. I've won like two.

58

ST. Okay. How do you do that?

BH. I don't know. The first award was just because of a submission—

ST. Yeah?

BH. —to a theater company that I had worked with before. There may have been nepotism involved. But I had worked with them before. And they boiled it down to, I think, like five or six finalists. And then they gave all of the plays to Sir Peter Shaffer, he read them all. And he picked the winner.

ST. What was it about?

BH. It's about a collection of scientists who are trying to pinpoint a whale that was launched into space.

ST. Ooh...

BH. It's called *The Whale and the Dog Star*.

ST. How did you come up with that idea? What's like sort of the seedling, just—is there a pattern or like a way in which you start something that you can trace for yourself as an artist?

BH. Most of them start on whims, you know, or it's just an image that I can't get out of my head, to the point where I have to explore it. So like, this one was just the image of a whale in space. And I was sitting with my friend on the train. And I looked over at her and I was like, "I can't get this idea of a whale in space out of my head." And she was like, "Why are you so weird?" And then after that, I started asking myself questions about it. Like, "Why is it there? Who put it there? What are they doing? What are they like? Why are they down here while that's up there?" The more questions I could ask about it, the more it turned into a little story. And I could ask you the same thing because you do so many pieces that are approached from so many different disciplines from—you know, not just the writing or devising standpoint or directorial standpoint, but from a technological standpoint. And many mediums too. So when you have an idea, where does it start?

ST. Usually it's because I'm angry about something, to be completely honest. *Iranian Girlfriend* was a piece that I'm still working on that had a reading here at Brick Aux. And I think I was angry because I didn't fit in with my boyfriend at the time's family. And so I just started writing about it. But there's also a piece that I'm working on that is more "technologically-based"—currently called *U + ME @ the edge of the earth*—and it's about time-travel, nothing to do with anger, it's about memory and time... so. I'm interested in the way that memory functions for people ...how it might work for nations ...how we forget things. My partner and I are working, collaborating on it with AI, with artificial intelligence. More soon on that!

BH. That's awesome.

ST. And now I take it back to you. IKEA.

BH. IKEA, yeah, yeah...

ST. So I read online, that you explore "futures from a mythological perspective in [your] writing," but you also work with IKEA—or you did—or you have? SPACE10 is a research and design lab. Can you talk a little bit more about this experience and also a little bit more about your work as a creator of digital *and* live experiences, because you create multidisciplinary work and I am very interested in how that happens for you.

BH. Working with SPACE10 happened through an agency that I had been working with. Extrapolation Factory.

ST. Yes.

BH. They're a futurism firm that does futures designs and futures experimentation. And they do a lot of live incubators where they invite people to performances or immersive experiences that kind of help give them an idea of different potential futures. And I got looped in with them because A) I'm a lover of science fiction and exploring the future and I love to write from that perspective, and B) they just needed a writer at the time when we first started. So with the very first piece we did we were working for Ford. And we were writing—

ST. Ford? The car company?

BH. Yeah, yeah.

ST. Keep going. We're still on a date, right?

BH. Yeah, yeah.

ST. Because—

BH. It's going swimmingly.

ST. Thank God.

BH. And we were writing pieces, immersive audio pieces, for their engineers and designers to get an idea of what the world would be like in 15 years, for their new collection of like, electric trucks or whatever. And that went well. So then, yeah, we started doing a piece with SPACE10, which has since dissolved. I have no idea why. Could speculate all day long. But it was also very interesting because during the pandemic there were a lot of companies and a lot of people more interested in futurism than there are now, and I think it's because we couldn't tell what the world was going to be six months from now, let alone 15 years.

ST. Can you talk more about futurism because it's part of your practice, no? Or the way that you write?

BH. We really just pretend, honestly. Like it's—there is a lot of like graphing and mapping and projecting and looking at current technologies…but really, at the end of the day, we're just making shit up.

ST. Yeah.

BH. And we're like, "Wouldn't this be cool? Wouldn't this be interesting?" Or, "This feels like a natural progression of this."

ST. Like time. So that's not real either.

BH. I guess to me—

ST. Okay.

BH. —it is, in a way—

ST. Okay.

BH. —just not in the way that we perceive it.

ST. Go on.

BH. Because like, the idea is that time exists everywhere simultaneously. So, in a way, it exists. With sequential time, that's just the way that we interpret it.

ST. So what does that mean about history?

BH. That it's all happening right now?

ST. And it happened and it will happen?

BH. Yeah.

ST. Oh, God.

BH. And that we're all just swimming. We're just in a pool of history right now. You know?

ST. Oh, wow.

BH. Yeah, yeah.

ST. Like, The Exponential Festival happened nine years ago.

BH. Yeah.

ST. And it's happening right now.

BH. Yeah.

ST. And it never happened.

BH. But it's always happening.

ST. Jeez. Well, now I need a drink.

BH. Do you think you experience time more as a pool, as a soup?

ST. I think that moments in time, and being able to recall them, mean a lot to me.

THERESA BUCHHEISTER + LENA ENGELSTEIN

LENA ENGELSTEIN *co-created* all I want is what you want *with Jo Warren for the 2022 Exponential Festival. In addition, Engelstein appeared as a performer in works by Lisa Fagan ('19 and '20), Brendan Drake ('20), and Barnett Cohen ('23).*

THERESA BUCHHEISTER *is the founding Artistic Director of The Exponential Festival, of their theater company, Title:Point, and the now-defunct, former Exponential venue, Vital Joint. In late 2019, Buchheister became the Artistic Director of The Brick Theater, and in 2024 was honored with an OBIE Award for their work. Buchheister has directed, created, and/or performed in many shows presented by Exponential, including* Biter (Every Time I Turn Around) *('16)*, Chroma Key *('17)*, Everything of Any Value *('18), and* Sleeping Car Porters *('19), as well as curated the semi-annual salOn! variety series, among countless other creative contributions to the festival.*

LENA ENGELSTEIN. So I was supposed to be interviewing another Exponential artist tonight, Marissa Joyce Stamps, who unfortunately can't be here. And I got here at six. And Theresa said, "Okay, so actually, I'm just going to interview you," and I said, "No, I would like to interview you, too." And I actually think I should start.

THERESA BUCHHEISTER. Okay.

LE. Nic had said, just before we started, that this doesn't have to be a "postcard" for Exponential. But I do think, as it is the kind of throughline or the connector between all of us, I think it's a good place to start.

TB. Cool.

LE. And I think a good place to start is the start of it. So many people here have started festivals or spaces. And there's always an inciting conversation. I'm curious what was happening in that conversation, who was there, and why it didn't dissipate as an idea, how it came to actually happen.

TB. Well, one of the worst things about me is if I have a potentially terrible idea, I will do it. So basically, in 2015, my friend Eliza Bent had a show, *Toilet Fire*, that I missed because Title:Point's show, *Biter (Every Time I Turn Around)*, played at the exact same time. It's an issue that we all understand: when you're doing a show you miss everyone else's shows. At that time I was living in the East Village in this weird apartment that D.J. Mendel had but wasn't staying in. And so Eliza came over. I was chain-smoking in the kitchen. And we were drinking whiskey. And we were like, "What if we did a thing in January, so that I can see your show, and you can see my show? And then we can maybe ask Grandma," which was Peter Mills Weiss' company at the time, "and we could ask Darian Dauchan, and we could just ask some Brooklyn venues. We should do it in Brooklyn because all the January festivals are in Manhattan, but all the art I see is mostly in Brooklyn." And then the night just continued. And the next day, we were like, "We should actually do that. Let's talk to our collaborators." So that was when the decision was made. And I'm bad at naming stuff, so Eliza sent me a list of like 35 names. And this was while—

LE. Eliza's good at naming stuff—

TB. Eliza's great at naming stuff. And so we went with the name.

LE. So Expo began in a cigarette smoke-filled room, with whiskey.

TB. Yeah.

LE. That energy feels true still.

TB. Continuing the vibe. You have been one artist who is sort of unique, in that you've been in and a part of multiple Exponential shows. I'm curious what your first entrance into it was. What did you think it was? What did it end up being to you? And how has that evolved over time?

LE. I'm just aware that I never sit or talk like this. I'm a dancer, for people who don't know. My first entry into Expo was in 2018? Or 2019?

TB. 2018, yeah.

> (*The production* LENA *is referring to was part of Exponential's 2019 January season, but it's possible the company first visited the theater in the final months of 2018 in preparation.*)

LE. I was there with Lisa Fagan's *Red Carrots*. I just remember that the space felt sort of unkempt. There was a strange backstage that had a bunch of stuff back there. There was a curtain. There was a *backstage*, first of all! Those of you who've been there know that's not true anymore. And we just had an amazing time doing that show, and it was really exciting for me the next year to come back in 2020, when you, Theresa, took it over, and to see the space change. It was really transformed and cleaned up. 2018 was the first or second year I lived in New York. And so I had a perception still that spaces were there forever. And it was kind of the first time where I realized that spaces are rarely anywhere for very long. And seeing something change for the better was really cool.

TB. And that year, you were also in—so that was *Catches No Flies*, but you were also in *Community Exercises for Sanctuary Spaces* by Brendan Drake.

LE. Yeah, I've done five Exponentials. And this January will be the first January I'm not, excluding the pandemic. Unless someone...

TB. Anyone casting? So: you realized that spaces don't last forever and that they change with the people who are inside of them. I guess another question would be, did it propel you towards self-producing and creating in a different way?

LE. Definitely. I think that Expo offered me an opportunity not to be confined by dance. I think that showing up with experimental performance that was dance-based, and then arriving at a festival where no one cared about that, about what you were based in, or what you were going to do—and like, once you opened your mouth and started talking, or had sort of strange set pieces, they weren't asking you to reconcile that with being a dancer. And that gave me lots of permission, moving forward, both in the work that I made and in what I brought to other work. It just generally expanded my horizons in the way that experimental work can often do. Being in a festival where everyone was pushing at the boundaries of what they were doing, I felt very fortunate, because oftentimes dancers are hemmed in by what they think the boundaries are and where they "belong." And so I, very early on, was like, "I can do <u>that</u>. I can do *that*. I can do **that**. And I can call it all dance also, by the way." And I still do.

TB. Yeah, well, I think that there are also a lot of comedians that think that you're a better comedian than most comedians.

(*Affirmative "mmms" from the audience.*)

LE. And this is going to be in print, right?

TB. "The best comedian in Brooklyn."

LE. Thank you. And I think another thing that Expo offered me was that expanded sense of community, and of how people were considering me: comedian, actor—some people are like, "Oh, you're an actor," you know, and I'm like, "No, I'm not. No training whatsoever. You just are being offered a platform to see me in that way." I met my partner doing Exponential.

TB. It is a hookup festival.

LE. And only some of them last! And we really did. This is totally an aside from this conversation, but when we first started dating, we used to try and meet up in our dreams, and we would pick a place we'd both been, and for a month we were trying to meet up in The Brick dressing room, because we had both been there and we really knew it. Which I think is emblematic of the way the personal histories and artistic histories and collaborations weave through that space and the festival. Which takes me to my next question. Okay, running The Brick, starting Exponential, running Exponential, being who you are, I think you see the most work of anyone I know, at a range of levels. And I'm curious, as an artist, throughout all of that, how it impacts what you want to make, what you really *don't* want to make, and if you feel like you're really attuned to trends, because you see so much work.

TB. I mean, definitely a trend this summer was queer bugs. Like, everywhere.

LE. What is a queer bug?

TB. Everyone was making shows about various kinds of bugs, and various kinds of queerness. And also religion.

LE. Kind of guilty.

TB. Yeah, sort of guilty. But I mean, threads—it's like comparative theater-going, you know? You start to recognize connections between things, but that only *you* were recognizing, because it's only my experience. And that feels really special. And being from Kansas, where my only options were seeing Christ crucified every Easter as a play, it's really expanded what I get to experience. I think living here, the greatest thing is having too many options. And sort of being overwhelmed and being sad when you can't make it to everything. On Saturday, I'm going to Ilana Khanin at Prelude, and then I'm going to Gillian Walsh because Neal Medlyn is dancing in that show, at 6pm at Danspace, and then here at 7:30 pm, for (*Exponential alum*) Josephine Simple, doing *This Show is My Funeral*. And I don't know how I'm gonna do it, but I'm gonna do it. And those are my favorite days! And then that day becomes its own story.

LE. Right.

TB. But it also spoils me a little bit because a lot of times—when I was 22 and making stuff, and I look back at videos, I was like, "What I'm doing is so original, and no one's ever done this"—I try to recognize that I get to see stuff all the time. And that's my experience, and everyone comes into every situation from not that place. And so the value of what somebody is doing for them might be different than what I'm perceiving. So I always think that that's an interesting conversation as well.

LE. And how do you feel like it impacts your work, and Title:Point's work?

TB. Makes it harder to rehearse!

LE. Because you're busy?

TB. Yeah. But it doesn't make me feel like I can't make stuff, it doesn't make me feel like all the ideas have been done, or that I have nothing to offer. Scheduling is the worst part of anything, including this festival, including the space, including existing. So Title:Point sort of pivoted to doing film stuff during the pandemic because scheduling was hard, and many of our collaborators moved, and some had kids, and all of these things made it a little bit harder to figure out how to do plays in the way that we used to. But I think that is important, because *no one* should always do plays the way they used to. You should always be changing how you're approaching things and who you're working with. And if it's not changing, then your show might be problematic! And it might not be relevant to anyone other than you. And that's okay. You can do that, too. But why would anyone want to be a part of *that* community? I don't know. But I will say that whenever I see something where I'm like, "Ooh, how did they do that? That's impossible. Don't tell me how you did it…but maybe tell me how you did it." That's really exciting, to figure out things—and then to also help younger people, when people ask, "How do I figure out the right blood recipe?"

LE. Right

TB. Come to me.

LE. Oh, yeah.

TB. I think you learn that blood recipe from years of trying and failing and getting stuff in your mouth and eyes that you don't want to. Or into your clothes, or on the floor that you can't get out. And then I'm like, "How can I do that more? How can I pull back and do it differently?" Part of the reason we did film is that our shows are usually disgusting in some way—we exchange bodily fluids or interact with each other in the space, and it was just too nasty to do without testing.

LE. Yeah.

TB. And making a safe space to do it.

LE. Yeah.

TB. So that will continue, but it will just change. And the things that are gross to me change over time too. So my final question for you is, what is something that you would like to do on stage that you've never done?

LE. What haven't I done up there? Oh, I would like to do something really punk, like really screamo, really kind of dangerous.

TB. Anyone casting? You'll be in a Title:Point show and I'll do that for you.

ELIZA BENT + JOEY MERLO

ELIZA BENT's Toilet Fire *was a founding production of The Exponential Festival in 2016, and was remounted for the 2020 festival.*

JOEY MERLO's On Set with Theda Bara *played as part of the 2023 Exponential Festival. The next year, Transport Group and the Lucille Lortel Theater presented a return engagement of* Theda Bara, *giving Merlo his Off-Broadway debut.*

This interview was conducted over Zoom.

ELIZA BENT. The last time that we Zoomed, you Zoomed into a class I teach, "Improv for Writers." You were being very professional, and I kept trying to make you be silly. Do you remember this?

JOEY MERLO. I didn't know you were trying to get me to be silly.

EB. Everything is harder on Zoom.

JM. Okay, Eliza Bent. How hae you found the process of moving from the traditional Greek-tragedy kinds of plays you used to write to stand-up comedy? Would you call *Penguin in Your Ear* a stand-up routine? What is it? How has it been for you to venture into something that's adjacent to, but different from, the kind of work you were making?

EB. I feel like I'm still processing what it all is. A choreographer here in Chicago was like, "I'd love to see your work." And I tried to send her the video of *Toilet Fire* only to learn that

Knud Adams deleted the one existing copy. That is on the record! We all have different relationships to technology. So this same choreographer saw *Penguin in Your Ear* when I did it in Chicago, and she was like, "Is that similar to your work? Or is it different?" And I was like, "Both." A lot of the work I've done has been me yammering away. But this does feel like a departure, it's more distilled. It's not as concerned with theatricality. And then somebody in the break room today at my job was like, "I loved your performance art." And I was like, "What are you talking about?" And she was like, "When you asked the audience questions that felt like performance art." And I thought that that was amazing and amusing.

JM. I did read that Knud deleted the only electronic copy of *Toilet Fire*, which made me feel very sad because when I found out that we were going to interview each other, that's something that I wanted to request. I think Nic Adams said that was one of his favorite theater experiences. And I've heard from other friends just how fun and funny that show was. And just looking at what was up on the Exponential website, in the language you used to describe it—as a "scatological liturgy" and instead of confessions, "conflushions"—I feel like that's a thread in all of your work, the wordplay and how you use language.

EB. Well, I mean, game sees game, Joey. You are also the king.

JM. I admire your relationship to language, which feels constantly inventive and also hilarious. So I was curious to ask you how you use language, how it's changed over the years, and who are the artists that have influenced you, or who have championed the way you use it in your work?

EB. I feel like I used to be really florid. With the very first play that I wrote in grad school, I was like, "I know! If I write it in Italian and then do this direct translation into English that'll help me not be florid." But it ended up being just a different kind of florid. It was an Italianized...Florid-ian... florid. And so—over time, and especially now doing the stand-up stuff, it's like, telling it plain. Knowing when to use a term like (*in a melodious High Tider dialect*) "More salubrious in the boudoir" versus "Sex is better."

JM. Uh huh.

EB. And how has that been for you? What's been your language journey?

JM. I will answer that. But first I wanted to mention that, you know, as you're saying these words, you're doing it in a funny voice. And obviously, a transcription won't be able to capture the hilarity of that voice. I feel like our relationship is one of funny voices and leaving voice memos and coming up with these zany characters. And so to me, it also feels like how the language hits or how you shift gears is so inherent to you, Eliza, to your personality, and to you as a performer. And so, in a way that feels really special, whenever I've seen anything of yours, it feels like, "I don't know if anyone else could do this." And I don't know if I'd want to watch anyone else do this. Part of what makes it so special is that you are doing it. And even if you're playing a character, there's a kind of crafted clown that shows up. Is that a weird thing to say?

EB. No. But it's just interesting to hear you say that about me because I could, would, will say the same thing about you. I mean, I always think about you coming to Brooklyn College, speaking to my class and me asking you to do your Marisa Tomei tale. And not only did you give us the tale, you leapt out of your chair. You fully embodied it. Sometimes there are different speeds of writers. And something that I really appreciate about you, Joey, is there's an exuberance and an aliveness to your energy that includes leaping out of a chair, includes leaving voice messages as, you know, (*in a Jersey Italian-American dialect*) Pasta e Fagioli-Auntie, Auntie Maria Assunta, Step-mama Nonna, and just this, like, soup of accents and voices, and a willingness to jump into character. I feel like being an adult who still has a sense of play is a pretty rare thing. And I feel like it's something you and I really do share, Joey.

JM. I see you as a kindred spirit in terms of our sense of play. And we both are actors, as well as writers, who are interested in improv. I think a play itself can feel more alive if I'm really letting myself go to a spontaneous place, and a place that feels more like improv, where it's not all completed and thought out and outlined—that what I might be able to capture is something that feels more alive and then can translate—that the text itself is living. And I guess that ties into what you were asking me in terms of my relationship to language. I think I've always been interested in sounds, and I think my writing has always been lyric because I'm interested in the sounds words make and how they might feel in your mouth, in a person's mouth, and how they feel in my mouth. And so words feel tangible in that way. I find it very satisfying to create musicality through language. When I'm writing, it feels like a score. There have been times when I've been very particular about what I'm doing with language and how I'm putting it together. And then there are times when I truly just kind of shut my brain off and allow it to be a more musical experience and just kind of let it all come out in whatever way it's going to come out. And I don't try to control it as much.

EB. It's so interesting to hear you talk about it because I was trying to articulate—this is a joke that I've made a bunch of times when I'm teaching but like—to encourage the students—like we all know what this kind of writing feels like: the hunched shoulders and the pounding on keys. Versus this kind of writing (*Eliza types joyously, bouncing lightly, smiling*) jazzy spontaneity. It can be hard to access that. When you're writing, Joey, what happens? Is it three hours? 20 minutes? What are the different rhythms?

JM. I used to write three to four hours a day. And then I would go for a run or do some physical exercise because I'd be so in my head. But grad school was so busy. I was reading so much—you're taking in so much—but also at Brooklyn College, we had to write a play a semester. And then we had Anne Washburn, and she had us do a shadow-self play—so then we're doing multiple plays a semester...and I just don't remember being able to stick to any schedule. So I was just writing, most of the time daily, but at all different times of day, for a few hours a day. When I wrote my last play, which was *On Set with Theda Bara*, I wrote that in like, five or six weeks, averaging like 10 pages a week, but I was also pretty sick and bedridden so that was part of it. I didn't have much of a social life at the time. And I was writing in a way that was very playful, and it felt like I could escape into this world and that was joyful, and something I really looked forward to. But you mentioned teaching and that's something else I wanted to talk to you about, because we both taught, and you're teaching at Northwestern. And I was curious to know how you've balanced your creative life with your teaching, and what worries you have in terms of the sustainability of that. Or how have you felt supported by the institution and by your students?

EB. I was washing the dishes earlier today and thinking about students, and then I was like, "Why are you thinking about students!?" Like, "Stop it!" (*As a cockney street urchin*) "Stop it! You're at home! You're not working!" But teaching isn't a job where you shut it off. You're always thinking about things to recommend to students or ways of talking about things. And it's also really interesting, now that I've been at Northwestern for a few years, to see students graduate. Over the summer, there was a student from when I taught at Brooklyn College, Erika Phoebus, who was at the Great Plains Theater Commons conference with me and it was incredible! She'd started that play in a class of mine! I was so moved, like—

JM. Wow.

EB. Yeah, to get to experience the play and see her as more of a grown-up and peer. What about for you? Does teaching feed you creatively? Sometimes I feel really exhausted by teaching.

JM. Yeah. I wasn't writing as much, but that also might be because I had just graduated grad school, and it was, you know, it was hard. It's hard to find the time. If you're juggling different jobs, and you know, you're grading papers— you have to really carve that time out for yourself. When I write and I go into that space, I kind of zone out, and then I'm not thinking about anything else. And that includes teaching. Then I'm really present with what I'm making. I taught a playwriting workshop at Brick Aux recently, and that was a wonderful experience. I didn't know how teaching this workshop would affect me. I was a little worried because anytime you teach something and you synthesize your own knowledge and then develop prompts and, you know, ways of passing knowledge along and passing tools along—when I think about doing that, I think about a reckoning that happens where you're confronting your own process and the tools you've been given, and you're needing to sift through that and decide what actually is useful. It was like a retrospective, in a way, going through all of the teachers I've had, and all of the methods and ways of writing, and then translating what's worked for me as something that might be useful to other playwrights. Ultimately it was inspiring because you see others take that information, those prompts, those tools, and they're generating material, and the material is exciting. And I'm so interested in the work that's being made and that all feels very affirming. And it's like, "Oh, yes—I have knowledge." When I've gotten stuck, I've thought to myself, "Okay, what would you tell a playwright who's taking your workshop? I try to listen to that inner 'Teacher Voice' that says: "Get out of your head, get out of this space of needing to solve everything, and return to a sense of play."

EB. Earlier today, I had to write something. I would rather have a tooth pulled, I'm so so dreading writing this thing. I set a timer, I did my little tricks. I put my phone into airplane mode but I still procrastinated with some other stuff. Then I was like, "You need to put a hat on. You need to wear a silly hat. The hat will help you focus and stay in character." Then I was thinking, (*in a voice like Richard Nixon*) "That's ridiculous."

JM. Did you do it?

EB. Yes! Of course!

JM. Did it help?

EB. Yes. I don't think anything that I wrote is usable in the soup, but the water's boiling.

JM. Can you put the funny hat on now?

(ELIZA *does.*)

EB. My "Stay Ready" cap. This comes from the company Pure for Men. Are you familiar with Pure for Men?

JM. No.

EB. No? It is a fiber product that a lot of gay men enjoy using to prepare for various activities. Clears you out. The person who made Pure for Men bought a home from my sister. She's a realtor and "Stay Ready" is Pure for Men's motto.

JM. Okay, let me show you my hat.

(JOEY *puts on a hat.*)

EB. Oh my God.

JM. It's the Emily Dickinson Museum hat.

EB. Aren't there like so many poems of hers?

JM. I've read all of her poems.

EB. Have you really?

JM. I've read a lot of her poems. And I was teaching at Amherst over the summer.

EB. Brag.

JM. You're from Massachusetts. Am I making that up?

EB. I am from Massachusetts. I was joking. You're not bragging.

JM. You have a gay hat and I have a Massachusetts hat, so does that mean—

EB. Our identities have blurred!

JM. Our identities have blurred.

EB. We are one and the same.

JM. So this was something I wanted to ask you. There's all this talk about how the Downtown theater scene is dying or dead. But then there's also this shift where work is being made in Brooklyn, and The Brick is very much a part of that. And so is The Exponential Festival—what are your thoughts on all of that? Do you feel like the "theater is dying" narrative is inaccurate?

EB. That's such a thorny question for me to answer because, like, a part of me died when I left New York. Like, I'm not there. Not to be maudlin, but I don't feel like I can really speak to if theater there is dying or changing or shifting because I'm not actually there. I can say that the theater that I have seen in Chicago has left me puzzled. But my relationship to the theater has changed. So I don't think it's dying. But I do think it's shifting and changing and morphing in interesting ways. I mean, Playwrights Horizons is doing solo shows this season. To me, that's a pretty massive shift in the larger, like landscape and ecology of—

JM. You mean, just because solo shows—

EB. Yeah. And they're Exponential Festival alumni—Alex Tatarsky, Ike Ufomadu—and Milo Cramer—but just like this—it's a giant LORT theater that's doing solo work.

JM. Hmm.

EB. Do you think that the Downtown has died? I mean Under the Radar was done…

JM. And now they're back.

EB. And it's going to be different. And it's great. I don't know. Erin Courtney lives here in Chicago, and I've heard her talk about 13P in so many different iterations, like coffees with different theater people. Do you think some things have to die for other stuff to—

JM. I wonder if the more interesting things are always going to be the things that lack resources because then it's the community making it happen. If it's a passion project for everyone involved, then maybe something more interesting is able to happen, and you're savvier with the resources that you have which may also, inadvertently, create experimentation. With those constraints, you're making something that's utilizing the inherent tools of theater as a medium. Nic, you're here.

NIC ADAMS. I'm sorry to cut you off midway, Joey. But I want to offer two things to wrap up. For Joey: Eliza was talking about you and your vivacity, and how great of a performer you are. David Greenspan is doing phenomenal work in *Theda*, and, as a thought experiment—is there a version of this production that you look forward to where you play those four roles, those four voices? For Eliza: Theresa did this live event a couple of weeks ago, where they outlined the genesis of Exponential, and your name was invoked. They recounted how a night spent discussing each other's shows led to this festival that's changed my life and changed a lot of artists' lives. So if you want to set the record straight, Eliza, about how that evening went, and how you remember it, I offer that to you.

JM. David is so specific and meticulous and came up with this whole gestural vocabulary for the play. At one point during tech, he was running late and I joked that I'd be his understudy. I got in the chair. And I was doing it, but really doing it like David, so it was really a David impersonation. That was fun but ultimately, I don't think I would actually enjoy doing what David's doing every night. And I think the play is built to be performed in many different ways and by many different actors. I'd be interested in seeing a version where a genderqueer teenager plays all the parts. I'd be interested in seeing a version where, you know, like, a 100-year-old woman is playing all the parts. But I'm not so interested in doing it myself... One of the reasons why I stopped acting so much in the first place is because, for a long time, I used acting as a way to express myself, especially when I was closeted as a queer person, and it was a way to escape my own reality and to create expansiveness. And I think once I accepted myself and then also came out and was accepted for the most part by my family, by my community, I became much more interested in getting to know myself. And writing plays allowed me to do that and to explore myself through character. I'm more interested in continuing that writing journey than I am in playing a part in my own play.

NA. Eliza, do you want to tell the story of how Exponential came to be?

EB. Yeah. I was mad, as usual. (*In a Mid-Atlantic dialect*) "Nobody had invited my play to happen again." I had missed something Theresa was working on. And there was this other play that (*Exponential alum*) Julia Sirna-Frest and Zoë Geltman had worked on. And I was just like, "We should do a thing!" Why not put these things on, like a consortium or in repertory? And we went to wherever Theresa was staying at the time, and we drank whiskey late into the night, and it was so fun. I remember thinking "Well, that's not gonna happen." It was immediately clear that Theresa wanted to invite everyone and that I was much more interested in wielding power and being exclusive, and saying no to people. But then, as time went on, and as I learned more about what Theresa was up to, and as Nic got involved, I remember a feverish text exchange with Theresa. I was in Boston, and I just remember Theresa being like, "What are we gonna call this thing?" And by that point, I knew that Theresa was running with it, and I was but a whisper in the wind, but I did come up with the name Exponential Festival. Which, in many ways, there's a poignant irony given that the COIL Festival is done. American Realness? Finito. Under the Radar? Croaked, now reborn—having its resurrection time. But there was a heyday of winter arts festivals and trying to get those APAP (*Association of Performing Arts Professionals conference*) people to attend.

But I think probably touring has changed a lot too. And (*in a low British dialect*) the landscape...the landscape.

CRISTINA PITTER + BAILEY WILLIAMS

BAILEY WILLIAMS *and* CRISTINA PITTER *both presented their work with Exponential for the first time in 2018, with Williams' play* Buffalo Bailey's Ranch for Gay Horses, Troubled Teen Girls and Other: a 90 Minute Timeshare Presentation *and Pitter's performance piece of ritual, storytelling, and poetry,* Decolonizing My Vagina. *Williams would go on to present her play with Emma Horwitz,* Two Sisters Find a Box of Lesbian Erotica in the Woods, *in the 2024 Exponential Festival, and Pitter would return in 2019 with* cracking open, *co-created with Serena Miller, and in 2024 with* ixchel [we are still here, remember this medicine]—*a performance installation and ceremony.*

CRISTINA PITTER. I was just immediately thinking of gay horses, so ...

BAILEY WILLIAMS. Gay horses told me to start. And I listened.

(CRISTINA *laughs.*)

BW. Tell me the story about how you started making art. What gave you the push? Who encouraged you? Who did you look towards? Who were your mentors?

CP. What a beautiful beginning. I have been making art, been drawn to art since I was very young. Originally, I wanted to be an illustrator. I was obsessed with being able to draw cartoons, and still life. There was a moment where I dedicated a whole sketchbook to all Disney characters, like being able to just look at it and draw it and get it refined. And that kind of went on the back burner because it's expensive. I grew up with very limited resources and knew like, oh, "For me to pursue this, I have to take a step back." I couldn't go into it in the way that I wanted, which is, I feel, the case for art in total, whether it be visual, performance …but yeah, kind of led with drawing first. I have always loved music and dance and poetry and storytelling in all forms. So that was the beginning. And I always had support from my family.

BW. Are they artists?

CP. They…are…not. I had to really think about that. My dad plays guitar. So—

BW. Oh! But that's—

CP. Yeah. So like, yes, they have artistic leanings. I don't think they would call themselves artists. I think they have artistic souls. I like defining things, and also completely eradicating definition. So here we are. I'm thinking of my third-grade music teacher now, Mr. Sepulveda, who was so cool. And instilled in me a deep appreciation, and to always be earnest in what you do. I don't think I have particular mentors—

BW. When did you turn to more theater, performance, dance?

CP. Yeah. Middle school.

BW. Oh!

CP. Bonkers. I moved around a lot as a child and even as a young adult. And there was this two-week program, Brentwood School District out in Long Island, and you had to choose between doing a band concentration, a musical theater/chorus concentration—maybe a third thing that I'm not remembering—but I chose the theater, and I remember just being so enthralled and infatuated and very aware that what we were singing was like, "Ummm I don't think this is age appropriate. But I love it because my hormones are RAGING." I'm talking *Pippin*. I'm talking *Sweet Charity*. Like, why are twelve-year-olds saying, "Hey, big spender."

BW. It's very sexy, Fosse...

CP. "Spend a little time." Trouble! So stupid. And how formative.

BW. Yes, of course.

CP. "I really like this. I'm gonna keep doing it." And so I did it in high school. I moved to Florida and yeah, it was a cool drama club. Why is it called a drama *club*? I don't understand.

BW. It creates a gated sense of scarcity. "This is something more people would do if they could. But they can't."

CP. "It's only for us true artistes of the theater!" I hate it.

BW. When did you start making your own work?

CP. It was high school. Wow. I'm really rolling through, like, film tapes of my life. Yeah, we had an assignment where we had to pick a song. There were choices that our teacher gave us. And we were separated into groups—one person would be the director, and/or writer, and then there were actors. And I was both the playwright and the director, and the song that we chose, or maybe was like left over out of the draw was, Reba...wait, no, I'm forgetting her name. It's... wow, I should know this. (*Singing*) "I can't make you love me if you don't. You can't make your heart feel something it won't." What—who are you!?

BW. We'll find out when this is published.

CP. But that song. I was like, "Oh, this is deep. This is tragic." Pain and great. And so I wrote a play about, oy, like familial trauma. What up, self-reflective! The alcohol abuse... how that plays in. And relationships between parents and siblings. And yeah, that was the first thing that I made.

BW. That's so interesting... you've been writing about family and ancestors since the beginning.

CP. Yeah. Wow. WOW. What a—wow. I have not thought about that in years. I'm getting chills down my spine. Thank you for that question.

NIC ADAMS. Bonnie Raitt.

CP. Thank you!

BW. Ah!

CP. I was like, "It's not Reba!" I'm just thinking red hair. And they both have red hair.

BW. I was like, "That doesn't sound like Reba." It's a little bit more...schmaltzy, I think. I love her.

CP. I'm thinking about childhood now. Yes, what was the catalyst for your way into the arts? And is it something that you found very naturally or something that grew upon you?

BW. I'm really not sure. My family are also not artists.

CP. Mmm. Interesting.

BW. They're jocks, and entrepreneurs, and gamblers.

CP. The trio, the magic trio!

BW. Sometimes all at once. Nobody in my family does anything like this. But my best friend Maria's mother was an actor. I thought she was the most glamorous person alive. And Maria went to New York when we were in third grade and came back and was like, "I just saw the most amazing musical in the world. It's called *Cats*." And then my mom got me the VCR tape. And I watched it, and I was like, "This is it. This is the thing for me, by me, to me, I will be—

CP. The cat?!

BW. The cat! "I will move to New York! I'll become a cat! I'll be on Broadway!" And so that was the catalyst.

CP. Wow, what a beautiful word. The catalyst was *Cats*.

BW. On the VCR tape. And then I just truly never shook it loose.

CP. And how wonderful. That you did not.

BW. But I did discover that, unfortunately, I can't sing or dance. And to be a cat, you actually do need to sing and dance. So I had to pivot.

CP. Pivot into the experimental.

BW. It would have been easier if I could sing and dance, but you know what? That's okay.

CP. Because you can sing and dance.

BW. Yeah.

CP. Just not for—

BW. Just not well.

CP. —what they want. And that's okay.

BW. I was looking through the script of *Decolonizing My Vagina*, and I was like, what special people! It's Starr Busby, it's nicHi Douglas. And the trio of you! So I was hoping to hear about that collaboration, and your favorite collaborators who you make work with.

CP. Oh, wow. Yeah, they are so present in my heart. I just had the beautiful honor of seeing nicHi douglas' (*pray*).

BW. I saw it too. It was beautiful.

CP. Medicine. Beyond. Yeah, I try not to put things into favorites because I'm actively working against hierarchy. I feel like I hold everything in the space of like, "These are all people who I enjoy." And some relationships feel a little more intimate. I would say that about nicHi, Starr, and director Jordana De La Cruz, like there's such a deep—I feel so seen by them, and always want to collaborate with them, collaborate with Elinor T Vanderburg, who wrote *BLOODSHOT*. Oh! I'm thinking of all the beautiful, beautiful black femmes and women, because I didn't have that growing up. And so I find myself gravitating towards them to be seen, and to receive them, and to see them as well. I'm thinking about Charly Evon Simpson, Colette Robert, Akyiaa Wilson, like all these incredible folks I've had the privilege of either collaborating with in my own work, or being in their work and these ensembles. It's really special.

BW. When you start building something like *Decolonizing My Vagina,* do you come in with a strong sense of the song and the dance? Or is that like a space where you have an openness...?

CP. A bit of both. I had the poetry for a long time. And I had all these vignettes, like, "These are things that I know are tied together. And I don't know the space in between." Jordana helped me find that so incredibly. And knowing where my impulses and instincts were, but—I didn't quite have either the vocabulary, or wasn't far enough removed to make it. Hence bringing in nicHi, hence being connected with Starr. And to think, "Oh, yeah! The music that I'm hearing, you have already made it happen in your own right. What happens when we come together?" It's really incredible. I nearly think of the same questions because I have *Buffalo Bailey's Ranch* in my head. I want to know: your collaborators! I would love to know *how*, *where* that was born from.

BW. Oh, it was actually crucial to starting to make work again. I didn't write anything for a while after I graduated college. I was working for an agent. And when you work for an agent, your mind becomes filled with the work of other people, which is really positive in lots of ways.

CP. Always!

BW. I loved working with all of those artists and seeing so much theater, but it really left no room for my own work. So I was getting drunk at a birthday party in 2016 or something. Derek Smith and Alex Rodabaugh were there. And I had been posting manically on Facebook as Buffalo Bailey, sort of inventing the character in real-time...I don't really know what that was. It was something I felt I needed to do at the time because I was feeling not creative. And I guess it started just coming out that way.

CP. Built up for so long.

BW. I felt very trapped by "Bailey Williams, Agent." I was like, "I need to be Bailey Williams, Horsewoman" in order to make art again. I needed this shadow self as like an exit ramp from my life.

CP. Yes.

BW. And so at the birthday party, Derek and Alex were like, "Have you ever thought about making your weird Facebook posts into a show?" And I was like, "Will you guys make it with me? I'll never make it by myself."

CP. What a beautiful invitation for building community, to bring your dream and your medicine to life.

BW. Yeah.

CP. I love that.

BW. It was really fun too. We had some material from the Facebook posts, then we had a bunch of meetings that winter-into-spring where we just sort of talked about what we were obsessed with. And like Alex was really obsessed with the housing crisis and the mortgage foreclosures and stuff like that.

CP. Yes.

BW. So we had this crazy meeting where we sat in front of my computer and read the Wikipedia article about the housing crisis out loud because all of us are dumdums. And then we watched *The Big Short* and kept rewinding the part where the lady explained everything from the bathtub. We were just like, "Okay, so you get a loan, and then...?"

CP. How does housing work?

BW. Yeah, that was the longest part of the process, trying to understand what a mortgage is.

CP. And then be able to utilize that information into "Cool, what are the theatrical ways of...what are we doing?"

BW. Yeah, yeah. That's so important to the creative process.

CP. The dramaturgy!

BW. Exactly.

CP. And then be able to know, "Okay, this is based in some fact. How do we explode from there...onto a ranch?"

BW. Onto a ranch! How do you devise a ritual?

CP. I think about elements that come up when you think of ritual, and then try and formulate, like "Cool. What is this ritual for? And"—much the same—"Where is there room to explode from what the—" What's the word I'm searching for? A common place? Like, okay, when you smudge a room, you make sure there's a window open, and you make sure that you are articulating what you want to cast out. And you also have to call in what you want to come back in and put in that space and body and spirit and be able to have that, like "This is the base ritual that I know, factually"—or the dramaturgy of it. And then explode it from there, like "What other elements can be fantastical, theatrical, heightened," and yeah, I kind of go from there.

BW. I love that. Having a base ingredient, or a structure, and you're like "Okay, how do I play within this structure?"

CP. Yeah. Having a—¿cómo se dice?—having a structure so that chaos can reign beautifully within and inside that structure. Speaking of structure, I am so curious to know how you would want to build your actual ranch.

BW. Oh...

CP. Yeah, because I was visualizing it. Like what is the sanctuary for...etcetera.

BW. You know, in the script, the ranch is 90 minutes from New York City. I think probably not that. So starting from a "what I don't want" perspective...my ideal ranch? Say this question to me in a different way.

CP. I want to make sure I'm saying the full name ...*Buffalo Bailey's*...excuse me. I literally have to look this up really quickly. (*Sings*) Thank you.

BW. Once I said the name of the show incorrectly *in the show*. And that has haunted me since, so...really good lesson to make your titles shorter.

CP. *Buffalo Bailey's Ranch for Gay Horses, Troubled Teen Girls and Other: a 90 Minute Timeshare Presentation.* Timeshare. Okay. Should you do the show again, or make it in real life, how would you build your ranch?

BW. I probably wouldn't try to do as many things as Buffalo Bailey was trying to do to, you know, have the gay horses and board them and fight wolverines and also therapize troubled teen girls, I think that's probably a really suspect industry.

CP. Especially, the hindsight.

BW. I think it was suspect in the show, but I think we're learning more and more about these sorts of horse ranch scams for teens. Think we gotta leave that out of that. And *Other*? I would still welcome all *Other* to my ranch. I wouldn't structure it like a nonprofit, but I don't know if I'd be as money-grubbing as Buffalo Bailey is.

CP. It *was* the shadow self. Is there something that you learned in the process of making *Buffalo Bailey's Ranch* that really stood out to you, in your process that still resonates and perhaps influences the way you make work now?

BW. Since it was the first show that brought me back into making work, the piece of it that has really stuck with me and been pivotal to my practice is the joy of creation and having fun, and making things with people you love. I'm not doing this for any other reason, to be honest. It's to connect with the people I love and the people around me and to have a blast doing it. And if you can't do that, then why?

CP. What's the point?

BW. The rewards are so little even at the most advanced levels—it's like, find the reward somewhere else.

CP. Yeah.

BW. What about you?

CP. Oh, same. I've been thinking a lot about the things that delight me. And operating from that place. And how, even though I may know it psychologically, how easy it is to get tied up in the "Oh, let's make this deadline (*grunts*) let's make this like (*grunts*)—"

BW. "This has to be the best piece!"

CP. Yeah! Art takes time! I've never cared about perfection. I know that I am constantly trying to negate those pressures that are put upon this industry and, truly, the world. So yeah, operating from a place of joy and delight, being in process, staying present with that. Really just doing it for myself and trusting that what is being provided for me will resonate with other people even if I can't see it or feel it.

BW. Absolutely.

CP. To know that it lands and to name—name the damn thing. Yes. There's so much power in being simple, like, "No, this is what I want. This is what I'm saying. This is what I'm doing. I hope you receive it."

BW. Do you have any tactics for keeping the noise out? Like the bad industry noise?

CP. I state very clearly, "Oh, this is bothering me today." And I breathe and go. And I know that's not the end-all be-all.

BW. Yeah.

CP. And I know that our current society wants to fall into those trappings. I'm not gonna let it because I think I'm too damn good. I think *we* are too damn good to allow ourselves to succumb to that bullshit.

BW. No scarcity model. It's a trick! It's a trap!

CP. It's a trap! And to hold the whole. To hold these many truths at once. We are desperately seeking resources that we do not have—and we have an abundance.

NA. I have a question that I'd like to hear both of you answer. Because I think you'll answer it in very different ways. Whenever I walk into either of your theatrical spaces there's always this huge amount of energy. And sometimes I think about that as "audience experience." And sometimes—as you're talking about smudging a room I'm thinking, "Right, there's also this very ancient thing happening here." Is audience experience something that occurs to you early in the generative process? Halfway? After the fact? When do you start thinking, "When people enter this space, what is it gonna feel like?"

BW. From the very beginning. Yeah. I'm very interested in the audience and very invested in what they're experiencing from moment to moment. And theater is so short! As a time-based medium, you have from the moment the audience hears about the show to the moment they stop thinking about it, but you only have a little control over that period of time. And you can sort of take control starting with the marketing, which I think affects how people walk into a space and what expectations they hold. So I think about the marketing quite early, embarrassingly enough. I'm like, "What are the things that are going to draw people into this? How silly am I going to be? How elusive? Am I going to start promoting this on my Facebook several years before the show?" And then the minute they walk in the door, I want people to have a good time. I want there to be drinks, I want there to be music, I want there to be a vibe. I think it's so important, and it's the thing that theater fails at in sort of an inexcusable way. I don't want to name names, but is there any place less welcoming than some of our most lauded theaters?

CP. Absolutely.

BW. The drinks are too expensive. There's no music. It's cold. Like the lobby doesn't have any *seats*?! It's just crazy. So I think about it constantly.

CP. Constantly, yeah. I think about it from the beginning, primarily from an environment aspect. I'm very bad at marketing stuff. Like, I will do it and be fine, but I don't think about it until a week or two before. Like, "Oh, yeah, maybe I should, yeah, I should post about this. Can anybody help me make a sign?" Then I think, "How does the audience enter the space?" And then I know that I try—and sometimes fail—to generate that feeling of "Every step is a portal. Especially when you enter the theater space and want folks to be able to shed what they're carrying, and be present with what they're entering with. Whether that be through smudging, or taking in this space and all the weirdness that's happening. Giving them time to download what's around them before launching right into a piece. Yeah, and same, I want comfort. I desperately want to be able to feed and have drinks and cozy things at all times. And that's part of the ritual that I build, and knowing where it can *always* happen.

LEONIE BELL + LEE RAYMENT

LEONIE BELL *first presented her work as part of The Exponential Festival in 2020 with* Mamimumu. *In the years that followed, Bell began creating multi-media theater films that premiered on The Exponential Festival You-Tube channel, including* Einst träumte ich von dir: A Maybe-Myth of Runny Nuns *('21),* We Live to Die: The Grieving Widows Club: "Episode One" *('22),* "Episode Two" *('23),* and "Episode Three" *('25). She collaborated on Clay Moodey's* femme pathos *('18) and Nic Adams and Lee Rayment's* Corona Cam Show *('21) as an actor, and on Allyson Dwyer's* Arrow of Time *('23) as a voice actor and sound designer.*

LEE RAYMENT *is the creator of the cabaret performance series* "Stiff Drink!?" *with Dr. Eustice Sissy (Psy.D.),* presents…, *on which he collaborates with playwright and director* NIC ADAMS. *The two produced* Corona Cam Show *as part of the festival's digital offerings in 2021.*

LEONIE BELL. How did you find your mustache?

LEE RAYMENT. How did I find my mustache?

LB. Because it's a very specific mustache.

LR. It *is* a very specific mustache.

LB. I mean, it's very cabaret.

LR. Oh, it's very cabaret. Okay, so I think the question that I'm going to answer, which I'm going to also ask you, is: what was the performance or piece of art that changed the way you make your work?

LB. Oooh! I was going to write that down too.

LR. So here's the genesis of the character, Dr. Eustice Sissy. On a whim, Nic asked me, "Do you want to go see one night of Taylor Mac's *A 24-Decade History of Popular Music*?" And I was like, "Sure!" Didn't know who Taylor Mac was. Never heard of judy. Was completely blown away by the performance. I think we saw 1866 to 1896, a crazy few decades that no one knows anything about. So much so that I went back and got tickets for the next night.

LB. Cool.

LR. And after that show, I was like, "This is the kind of theater I want to do." And I started to mull. I love playing villains. But I thought, "What is a villain with a heart of gold?" So I came up with the idea. Dr. Sissy was the name and then I asked my friend Brian like, well, "What is his first name?" Eustice! Dr. Eustice Sissy. That's just ridiculous. That's perfect. And for whatever reason, in there, I knew, "This person has a mustache." And I think I got the idea from a friend of mine who does—she's not a drag king, but a little bit. I did a photoshoot with her. And—

LB. Which, by the way, I love your portraits.

LR. Oh, thank you.

LB. I want to hire you.

LR. She's one of those faces on my website! And she had these two triangles painted on her face, and I was like, "That's it." Because it just needs to be small. It doesn't need to be big. But that was the idea of the specific mustache, and then it just stuck. That's just eyebrow pencil.

LB. It's great.

LR. I sing with the New York City Gay Men's Chorus and last year we went to the opera and I wore the outfit that I generally wear as Dr. Sissy, but obviously without the mustache. And it was odd. I was like, "Something's missing…I feel naked and I don't know why." It's very weird how when you just put on that little bit of makeup—

LB. Yeah.

LR. —and all of a sudden, that's the thing that just like, pushes you into it.

LB. Totally. That's so cool.

LR. Yeah. So what was art that changed the way that you make art?

LB. I think someone that really hit the nail on the head is this guy Herbert Fritsch. He's a German director. He has this piece called *Murmel Murmel* and it's by a visual artist called Dieter Roth. And Roth also did all of the set design, which was essentially just mono-colored—kind of like an old Renaissance theater where the backgrounds would like—(*Leonie opens and closes her arms like curtains*) zzzzhooop! zhooop! zhoop! zhoop!

LR. Okay.

LB. And then as part of the accompaniment, there's a live musician, Ingo Günther—he has like xylophones, little bells, and he basically animates—

LR. The music?

LB. Makes music for what's happening on stage. And it just is amazing. But basically, *Murmel Murmel* is a piece where the only text is "murmel murmel," which means "mumble mumble." And the cast was like eight people of all sizes and shapes. I mean they were all white and yeah pretty ... pretty cis and white. But basically—

LR. Various types for Germany.

LB. They started appearing in duos and singing (*hands raised*) "Murmel! Murmel! Murmel! Murmel!" (*Hands lowered*) "Murmel! Murmel! Murmel! Murmel!" And they would, like, sing opera, and do it as monologues with these, at first, simple movement sequences that then started becoming this deranged, murmel-murmel-opera where they were basically out of breath. And, mind you, they're in like 50s outfits with horn-rimmed glasses and beehives, and little office skirts, but they're throwing themselves off the stage at this point—the music is happening—there are mats on the ground, they're pulling themselves up again—but they're in office attire, and I feel like the chaos and the humor of looking insane and doing this text but with such commitment and like—the beat work is, of course, very important.

LR. Right, right, right.

LB. And this director has done other pieces like that, where it's always a chorus or an ensemble of characters that are carrying us through this wave of highly specific chaos, a humor that's not due to a verbal joke but just everything that you are in your body—everything you're exerting—

LR. Yeah, yeah, yeah.

LB. And the fact that you're out of breath is just magnificent.

LR. Hearing that story and then knowing your work, that completely makes sense.

LB. And I love wigs, of course.

LR. Oh, yeah.

LB. Yeah. I feel like the videos and the cabaret I saw—was that at Vital Joint?

LR. Did you see that at Vital Joint?!

LB. Well, I watched the videos.

LR. That was at Vital Joint. It was—God, it was like 2018?

LB. Aw...R.I.P.

LR. Yeah, I know. R.I.P. When I was watching your stuff—I feel like your work is a combination of Wes Anderson, Terry Gilliam, with like a blast of Roald Dahl and like Quentin Blake, who was his—was Roald Dahl's illustrator.

LB. I love those aesthetics, yeah!

LR. That kind of—sketch and pencil lines.

LB. I feel like I generate material through either—yes, maybe writing a text here or there, though that's really random, where I'm like, "Oh, I'm moved!" I have a very chaotic writing practice. But in terms of creating characters or things—they often come from visual or physical impulses. I am a little bit of a beat-obsessor when I'm creating those types of scenes—that's when I know, most often, exactly what I want. Whereas with text and other aspects of the theater, I'm a little more like, "What am I—who am I—I don't know."

LR. Right.

LB. It's a different version of using my gut that's a little more nascent, right?

LR. Well, I think that where I see a line between both of our work is that both of us—and I don't know how apparent it is, but I know at least in our (*indicates Nic*) writing process—

LB. I wanted to ask you how you do that.

LR. It's really just me and Nic making each other laugh.

LB. Cool.

LR. It's like truly, the idea of play.

LB. Yeah.

LR. And seeing the piece that you just did at this year's ?!:New Works Festival I was like, "Oh, you're just—you're playing."

LB. Yeah, yeah, yes.

LR. That is so important for development. Yes, we'll tease things down. But often as we're writing, we're just making up jokes. And you do this as well—Nic and I talk about "putting a hat on a hat." It doesn't need a hat. But like, you're gonna put another hat—

LB. —and the hat is a wig. It's also a hat *for your* wig.

LR. Right?

LB. And THAT hat needs a wig!

LR. And there's a mustache somewhere?

LB. And the mustache moves around and around and around.

LR. 100%.

LB. The visual gags of it all are always going to be there, which also makes me think of Mel Brooks—

LR. Which is also, you know, big in my cultural canon.

LB. Yes! I was also really enjoying the different registers that you were quite effortlessly jumping in and out of—these pretty, what I would call contemporary Epic theater, but like, cabaret songs, that's the new Epic theater. Like the Greeks took on cabaret. It's very heartfelt. And there's no embarrassment, or shame, or any version of like, hiding yourself, because I feel like you have to go there. It's very Brecht, like, "show it off." And I feel like the character also has a bit of a—I don't know if misanthropic—that's something I thrive on, is playing misanthropic villains, or people who are cranky, but it's really funny and there's something sad underneath.

LR. Yeah.

LB. And clowns are sad. Or—there's something about like,

laughter and grief and comic-tragic characters who are mad. If you can be mean to the audience, and still have them—

LR. Be on your side.

LB. Carefree, you know?

LR. Yeah, yeah, yeah.

LB. And then also this thing where you don't know where the joke is? And like three seconds later, being like, "Oh, he just totally pulled a joke on you." That rings true. The misdirection of it all.

LR. It's funny because the first piece that I wrote, which was never completed—I was writing around the idea of how we reject the love that's in front of us. So in the original *Dr. Sissy* piece, what happens is that Dr. Sissy's partner, Marcus—you find out he proposed before the show—

LB. Excellent.

LR. And Eustice killed him.

LB. Oh my God!

LR. So, going on this idea of how do you reject the love that's in front of you, and what is the most extreme way that that could happen? If in the moment that someone is like, "I love you and I want to be with you" someone else's response is, "I hate you. I'm gonna kill you"—

LB. Yeah.

LR. Which, you know, it happened off stage, in a sort of...

LB. Greek way?

LR. Well I think initially we did it as a—it was like a puppet show.

LB. Ooh!

LR. Because Vital Joint had that door with a window to the back area, we mimed a ring and a finger and then like, a choking. It was very ...

LB. Very *House of Von Macramé*, the musical ...

LR. It was Nic's idea. Nic and I had worked on a show years before—we did *The Pillowman*.

LB. Oh. Is that McDonagh?

LR. Martin McDonagh, yeah. And we were like, "We don't have the budget to have a bunch of actors act out Katurian's stories." So they were all done through shadow puppets.

LB. I also love that you play with the *commedia* power dynamic of the servant and the boss.

LR. Yeah.

LB. Oh, and then I loved when you had the audience members mouth the scene while you were reading the text in Vital Joint. I just love those types of little devices—you never know what could happen.

LR. Taking it back to Taylor Mac: the way that Taylor woos judy's audience into doing just the wildest shit is so incredible. And it's a thing that I still want to work and push more. I think now a regular part of the show is Eustice's opening song, having arm-ography that he teaches to the audience and makes them do as an opening salvo. And it gets people into the mindset that, like, this is going to be wacky, you better come along for the ride.

LB. I wrote "gay nonsense," yeah. Thank you.

LR. Truly, gay nonsense. And actually, the credit for that phrase goes to Alex Hare, who we were working with. He was doing marketing for us when we did the Corkscrew Festival and he wrote that line. I saw him recently and said, "That will stay with this show, this character, forever, because that is truly what this is: gay nonsense."

LB. Yeah.

NA. I see a throughline. Ask her about nonsense.

LR. Yeah, well—I was—okay, what is your—what is your nonsense?

LB. My nunsense.

LR. Your nunsense. And nonsense.

LB. Well, I just put in an order for eight nun habits, so ...

LR. Amazing.

LB. And two more of the collar and the headpiece. Because I decided I need lots of nuns in my next show!

LR. You know what I ...the ...I think that the question I was thinking of is, when you have all of these characters, what is the way that you track and remember them? Is it like, "For this character, I put this costume on and that's how I remember"? Is it a physical pose? Are you writing these things down?

LB. I usually start with one character who comes naturally.

LR. Yeah.

LB. For *The Grieving Widows Club*, I started with Winnie, who was this grumpy maid. Again grumpy-grumpy-grumpy, grump-grump-grump. I don't know why I'm so into grumps, but I am. There's something about them.

LR. Local Grandma (*the name of* LEONIE's *production company*).

LB. Yes. I'm like, "There's more to you than being a grump! But what is it??"

LR. Right, right.

LB. So Winnie is a grumpy maid. I created this piece for ?!:New Works 2019 and in it, I give envelopes with instructions to audience volunteers, and they start creating a party for me while I appear with various trays. And throughout the party, they're doing their instructions. And they also do stuff like put on silly glasses and do a synchronized dance with me. But basically, the premise is that Winnie hates her madame, her mistress, and murders her in the end.

LR. Amazing.

LB. I did this piece with audience interaction which was quite fun. And at the end, I'm covered in chocolate cake and stuff. And then that started turning into this show called *The Grieving Widows Club*, where I was like, "Oh, I'm gonna play the madame, and then I'm gonna"—I need another maid to balance out Winnie, the uptight maid, the more proper maid, she takes her job really seriously. And she's also a playwright, so in the community maids' theater she's a really scary dictator. I like the idea of people just losing their shit in certain spaces of their life.

LR. Yeah.

LB. And how diverse we are inside. Like me on my bike. I hope nobody sees that, ever, because it would change your opinion of me, but maybe you also have that person inside of you?

LR. It is driving. I have only driven through Manhattan once and it was a couple of weeks ago, and I was—

LB. Unhinged!

LR. I wasn't unhinged but I—someone pulled out in front of me and I was like, "What the hell?" My friends had to remind me, "You're fine. You need to calm down." I just realized, "This is not a good look for me."

LB. It's true what they say, that you become insane. So I guess I started with those characters, and those I know quite well, and then I make other characters who fill in the events that I imagined, or the scenes—then I just make up some shit that probably will never be repeated and I just do it however I feel. I'm pretty irreverent with dramaturgical things like that. But I also think if I had a bigger budget, and if I put more effort into actually getting funding for this, it could be a different experience. But I'm interested in completing this little trilogy in the manner I started it, which was in my house, doing everything myself, which is a little shitty sometimes, but I think just committing to that, and seeing what will come out, is a great start to then figure out what I might like to do in the future in that medium. Like how do you do that? Because your video was so polished and funny and so clear.

LR. So Nic and I, since we've been working on this character and this world for many years, like—we have a backlog of information—

LB. I can't wait for the retrospective.

LR. There is a timeline that exists in a database that I made, of all the events that are unwritten. Or like, we wrote this piece, but this little gobbet we didn't use points to how these theater projects that became video projects become playgrounds for the secondary and tertiary skills that we have.

LB. Yes! And they're very beautifully amateur, at least on my end, but I think trying new things is good for my brain.

LR. I did video stuff back in high school. It's a thing that I've sort of developed on the side—

LB. You probably know Photoshop really well—

LR. Yeah, yeah, yeah.

LB. Being a photographer...

LR. Relatively well. You know—I think—for *Corona Cam Show* I taught myself Adobe After Effects to do all the like, the "Dancing Tobies" in the music video—

LB. It was excellent.

LR. Thank you. It was so much fun. Nic, at one point said, "You've created a Boschian landscape."

LB. That's so good!

LR. That's the best compliment.

LB. That's really nice.

LR. But that's also the other part of the worldbuilding that I love. For the Corkscrew festival, where we made a podcast, they told us, "We're gonna make a webpage to put this on." And I just like…designed a whole webpage.

LB. That's so cool. It's like the German term, "Gesamtkunstwerk," when everything is in some way cohesive—the aesthetic and the choices and everything around it.

LR. All of this work that I do, it's like, "Oh, I get to fulfill my graphic design itch while also doing theater."

LB. Yes.

LR. How did you develop your visual style? Because it is so playful.

LB. Well, Terry Gilliam I love. I also love Edward Gorey.

LR. Oh!

LB. His brain and just his stories and his characters, there's something so—again—dark, tragic, funny, humorous—I think I'm very attracted to that. I just started making short stop-motion animations during the pandemic—I glued my phone to a pot and—

LR. And that's how you did it.

LB.—on my bed where I like clamped it to a stool and—

LR. Amazing.

LB. It was great. For a long time—I've drawn postcards quite regularly and just sent them to my friends because I love drawing little landscapes—it's my visual arts satisfaction. And I feel like the postcard stuff has transferred—I love making stencils and stuff. I feel like these types of graphic arts have made their way into my stop-motion animation. I just use iMovie and free websites like Photopea. I'm working on improving, but I also recognize that if you try to do everything at once, you can only be so good at things.

LR. Yeahhh...

LB. So I tried to set my framework to like: do it in your house, do it in two to four weeks. The script I write beforehand, but then I kind of improv. What about you?

LR. Our process is different every time, so—I think we will try to write something hopefully for an upcoming Exponential. But the process, it really depends, it's me and Nic, meeting up at a coffee shop, and making each other laugh without trying to make too much sound. Because sometimes you go to coffee shops, and they're like, oppressively quiet.

LB. Yeah, truly!

LR. Oh, here's a question. I'm very much a top-down—I need to know the structure of what I'm doing. And then I can fill in the bits. Nic is a bottom-up—and it sounds like you are probably more of—

LB. I think, yeah, like bottom-up.

LR. Like, you can play with this and put this together and do this...?

LB. Yeah, I definitely enjoy that. Because otherwise I feel a lot of pressure. But of course, when the time comes you just got to get to it. Make a thing and then like: strong and wrong, baby.

LR. I appreciate that because that is not a mindset that I have. I will do something, but there's going to be so much thought in the thing that by the time we get there…there's certainly play there, but there's been a lot of thought and time and pondering, "What does this mean?" Before I can sit down to write something I have to know, "Well, what is this about? What am I writing about?" I want to write a show about *something*. And if I don't know the something that I'm writing about, well then it's not going to—

LB. Right! Rather than having the something reveal itself to you.

SALOMÉ EGAS + ELLPETHA TSIVICOS

ELLPETHA TSIVICOS *and her collaborator Camilo Quiroz-Vazquez produced a short film,* Night Descends on Svalbard, *for the 2021 digital Exponential Festival.* SALOMÉ EGAS *first presented her work,* Reflejo, *as part of the 2020 festival. Since then, Egas has presented a short film,* Zurciendo Retazos *('21), and a live work of dance-theater,* Más que un Pétalo *('24) with Exponential.*

ELLPETHA TSIVICOS. So I was looking at the two shows that were part of Exponential—the 2020 and then 2021. I'm assuming in 2021 you planned for it to be digital, right?

SALOMÉ EGAS. Yes.

ET. And it's so crazy because 2020 was right before—it was January.

SE. It was literally that January.

ET. Yeah. So tell me what they're both called.

SE. So the 2020 one is called *Reflejo*, which means reflection.

ET. Yeah.

SE. And the 2021 is *Zurciendo Retazos*.

ET. Okay.

SE. Which means darning pieces.

ET. Cool. I loved both of them. But the 2021 one, *Zurciendo*

Retazos, I thought it was so cool—it was like a cooking show.

SE. Yeah!

ET. It was so functional. What I liked about it—and the parallel that I saw in a lot of my work—is how functional the information that you were sharing in that piece was. That it was not only a story, but you also were secretly teaching people things. My favorite thing about art is secretly teaching. And I've been thinking a lot lately about these books I used to read when I was a little kid, because it keeps coming up in all my work. They were called *The Royal Diaries*. They were books about different princesses and royal figures.

SE. Like real life?

ET. Yeah. All of them were real people. But they weren't just Anglo royalty. They're also like, indigenous tribes. And Ka'iulani in Hawaii. It was taking actual things that happened, but these were their "diaries." So the diaries were fiction, but it was historical. It was trying to give these people life.

SE. Yeah, yeah.

ET. I'm like, "Now I know all about Hawaii." 1959, that's when it became a state. That's when the US overthrew their whole country. So I was learning things. But I was thinking I was just being taken on a journey. It's been coming up a lot because of the relentless wars that we keep having, and just kind of talking about geopolitics. And then I'm like, "Wow, it's funny how much that helped me understand history better than the way I learned it in school," because it personified all of the characters in the history books. But they were all women, the ones that I read, they didn't do it for men. That was a big tangent to say: while I was watching your piece, I was like, "This is fucking awesome because I'm learning something. I'm learning something that is passed down culturally, like dyeing fabrics, cooking, all these different things, sewing, darning. And what I liked about both of your pieces is that you're teaching people about your culture, your history, and your personal connection to it all, while telling a story.

SE. Aww. Thank you.

ET. I wanted to know how you started doing performance and theater. Just because I see so much of your culture and folk traditions in your work. And those things we don't learn at conservatories, you know?

SE. Absolutely.

ET. The same with my own culture. So I was curious about that. When you started doing theater, when you started making your own work, and how you got into that. And also how that correlates to when you came to America.

SE. I started doing theater and performance in Canada. I was born and raised in Ecuador. I started dancing since I was like, what? Seven, eight years old. I started then. And by the age of 15, I turned out to be a very good dancer. So I was able to tour with a youth company in Ecuador. We toured Latin America, and at one point—when you hit 15 years old in Ecuador, you have to choose a career.

ET. You have to have a quinceañera?

Ellpetha's recent show was an immersive quinceañera. They laugh in acknowledgment.

SE. I chose not to because at that point my dad was like, "Well, we have money to either give you a quinceañera or for you to go to a dance festival in Cuba." And I was like "Dance festival in Cuba! I'm going to do that!"

ET. What kind of dance were you doing?

SE. In our school, we were taught ballet as our foundation, but most of our work was contemporary and modern.

ET. Cool.

SE. Yeah. So I did that for the longest time. When I was 16, you were supposed to choose a career which, in Ecuador, it's very specific. It's either, you become a doctor and you do biology, or you become an architect and do physics—or an engineer—or you become a lawyer and you do philosophy. And I was like, "Oh, none of this seems close." The closest one was philosophy. And after one year, I realized I wanted to do a year abroad to see what the world is about. And turns out that I got a scholarship and ended up in Canada. And in Canada, at my boarding school, they did not have dance classes. They didn't have a dance program—or they had an after-school, but not a class. And the class that they had was theater. In my young brain, I was like, "Oh, it happens on stage, it shouldn't be that hard. It's bodies on stage. We do that with dance." And so I enrolled in the class and quickly realized, "Oh, you have to use a lot of words. It's very different." But having all the dance training made me feel very comfortable in my body. I do always have so much awe for what the body can do and how the body literally can hold trauma, hold joy. That was what let me become myself on stage when doing theater. And then I came to the US. I felt during my undergrad that I was not being looked at. Like I never was getting the roles, or the principal roles. I was always on the side. My accent was too strong—

ET. Was that dance?

SE. I was doing a dance-theater program.

ET. Your accent was too strong?

SE. My accent was too strong. And, you know, all the plays were pretty white. So I was never—I never fit within the canon.

ET. Yeah.

SE. So after that, I kind of felt very silenced. And I was like, "What happened? I've been an artist this whole time. Why can I not create anymore? Why do I feel so blocked?" And I think a big part of my transformation was coming to realize that I have to create my own voice. I have to put out my own voice. I have to rediscover that. And this is how, in my performance, I started going back into my ancestry, into who I am culturally, like, what are my roots, what are the stories that I want to tell, and start writing my own stories because no one else was doing it. That's how I ended up doing a lot of solo work and creating my own work. It was because I did not find it anywhere else.

ET. Yeah, I think we all have that story—

SE. Yes!

ET. I mean, not all of us, but a lot of us end up doing it. It's funny because I started dancing too, and I only was a dancer until I was in high school. And then I did my high school plays. So I was like, "Oh, it's like dance"—and this is free because it was just public school. And so—you've also been to some of our training workshops—

SE. Yeah, yeah, yeah! I love your trainings. Like, sometimes letting the body go is what liberates the mind and it helps you be present.

ET. It's true that there's so much inside our bodies, and they can do so much. But we do hold traumas everywhere, and you never really know where you're holding them. I mean, when I was in college, everyone was like, "You are ethnically ambiguous, you're gonna get so many roles." Then I'd go in for a part and I just wasn't anything that any of the parts were, you know? I'd get called in for Latinas and I'm not Latina—and there are plenty of Latinas in this country. You know, I'd get South Asian, but then I remember once a girl I went to college with was the reader in the audition. And I remember I walked in, and she saw me and she just looked like, so upset that I was there. But I was called in based on my photo. So I look South Asian. I look like a lot of different things. But I was like, I'm not South Asian. And she knew I wasn't. I wasn't pretending to be. I'm not Muslim, but I'm Middle Eastern. I'm not going to pretend to be Muslim and wear a hijab because it is a religious thing.

SE. It's not your belief.

ET. I'd go in for toothpaste commercials and they'd be like, "You're a little too exotic for this role." And I'd be like "Okay..."

SE. I'm sorry. I haven't been called exotic. But every time I hear it, my body twitches.

ET. It happens to me like once a week. People don't even realize. They try to say it nicely and they think—

SE. They think it's a compliment, too.

ET. They could be like, "You're disgusting" but they say "exotic." But I don't have it that bad. I love the way I look. I wouldn't want to be anything else. But that's why I started making my own work, too.

SE. I love that. I also was looking at your work ...*Night Descends on Svalbard*, right?

ET. Yeah.

SE. I don't know how to pronounce that word.

ET. I barely do too.

SE. I have so much admiration for your work, and the ability of creating joy that you have. I feel like, you know, what we were talking about in your trainings, using the body, the body has this amazing ability to create and heal and create fun. And that's one of the things that I was admiring—well, in *QUINCE*, obviously, you are really trying to celebrate that.

ET. Yeah.

SE. Like, how we get to celebrate joy, and joy for our community on our own terms. And when I was watching your short—it was for 2021 too?

ET. Is that when that happened?

NA. Yep.

ET. 2021? Yeah. That fateful day.

SE. Yeah.

ET. We filmed it during the, uh—we've got so many different words for it—when the Capitol was stormed, on January 6, the failed coup. That's when we were filming it.

SE. That's wild.

ET. Yes. So that's an added layer. That's where some of it came from.

SE. I think my question right now, it's a little bit thinking about the complexities of human joy, humanity, grief, and death. I think I saw a lot of those themes in your short, right? There's grieving—really, I mean, in such a beautiful, poetic way—also in different languages and gibberish that I absolutely love.

ET. She's (*performer Michelle Uranowitz*) amazing.

SE. I was like, "Yes! Tell me more!" Like I totally believe this is a language.

ET. I just have to tell you—every single one of her lines was written in English. And we were like, "You're gonna do this in gibberish." And she walked in and did that. And she did it so well that there were a couple of takes that we couldn't use because I couldn't stop laughing.

SE. Yeah.

ET. Because it was so good. And then if you see in the subtitles, how they match...they match! Those were her lines!

It was amazing. But that also was a thing about how we sound to other people who don't speak whatever language we speak. I mean, a lot of people speak Spanish in the US, but a lot of people don't. So it's like you're speaking in Spanish, and to someone who doesn't understand it you're just speaking gibberish.

SE. Yeah.

ET. So I wanted to put that in there too. Because to somebody who speaks none of the languages in the show, it all sounded like gibberish to them. You know?

SE. And I love that. In itself, you're answering my question, which is, you're dealing with death and grief and all these things like loneliness, what it is to be like, on your own, how do you deal with all these crazy, complex emotions, and yet there's like so much humor in just life. The different languages and the gibberish killed me. I totally believed she was speaking a language. I was like, "What language is it?" Because I'm actually pretty good at identifying, because I'm an immigrant, I use that skill a lot. I started listening, and then after a while, I'm like, "I'm not getting this." And then after a while, I realized, "Oh, my God, it's gibberish!"

ET. She said a lot of it was inspired by—her grandparents spoke Yiddish, but she never learned Yiddish.

SE. Okay.

ET. So it was part that but also, sometimes when I'm in Holland, on my way to Cyprus, and they play the "fasten your seatbelt" thing on the airplane, it sounds just like her gibberish. It sounds Dutch. Sometimes it sounds German, and sometimes it's Yiddish. Sometimes it's just silly.

SE. I want to know a little bit more about you. Like how did you end up here? And doing theater. Here.

ET. I was born in the US, but no one else in my family has left Cyprus, except for my father. My father is one of three kids only, which is a small amount for the village that I'm from—village life—they usually have a lot more kids, but my grandmother had a lot of miscarriages because they're farmers. There's no maternity leave or anything. So she lost a lot of kids. But he was a goat herder, my father, and they were subsistence farmers. My grandparents were subsistence farmers. Up until my grandfather died in 2019, they were still going to the fields every day, and they're really amazing people. So my father wanted to be a philologer, which is part of the philosophy department. He had gotten into the school of philosophy in Athens, Greece. And it's so funny because he's such a practical man. And my whole family is extremely practical because they've never had the opportunity to be anything but extremely practical. But then when I found this out, I was like, "A philologer?!" I imagined him like Belle from *Beauty and the Beast*, he would be in the fields and my grandfather would be like "Sava, get that book out of your hands!" And the goats would be running down the hillside. Because my father is a terrible farmer. He was clearly never good at it. His departure from Cyprus had to do with—I mean, a few things—but one of them was he was a terrible farmer. Also in 1974, Turkey invaded Cyprus. There was a huge war. They ended up occupying 40 percent of the island. It's still occupied. And the 10 years prior to that were just very, very violent. Civil war amongst—just people killing each other, the different communities. So he left as soon as he could, my father. And I'm sure it had a lot to do with living through multiple wars at a young age, which is something—you know, even though we watch wars, I feel really lucky that I didn't ever have to hide from bombs or anything. I mean things have gotten crazy in the US with gun violence, but anyway—so he was going to go to Greece and be a philologer, which is somebody who studies the specific language and syntax used in ancient philosophical texts.

SE. Oh, fascinating!

ET. Yes. It's really specific. And I'm wondering now if that would have led to a law degree or something, philologer—just because of what you said. Because you don't just study whatever you want there. You have a few things. And then someone told him there was farm work in South Dakota with wheat, which is a big crop where I'm from, in Cyprus, wheat. So he came to America to work in the wheat fields in South Dakota. And he met my mom in Astoria and stayed in the tri-state area. I'm always like, "Wow, I could have been me in South Dakota."

SE. Have you ever been to South Dakota?

ET. No. But they were like, "There's farm work," and that's what he knew how to do. So they met in Astoria, and my mom grew up in New Jersey. They got married, they moved to New Jersey, I was born in New Jersey—with dual citizenship with Cyprus—and my whole family has always been there, they've never left. They have no desire to leave their homeland, which I think is so beautiful. And I do think that one of the privileges I have as an American is the mobility to be able to do things. I'm not going to starve for a year if I leave my crops, because I have no crops. But my grandparents couldn't just come to America. I mean they did a couple of times when I was little, for a very short amount of time. All that to say, my mother put me in ballet class when I was three or four. She said I used to spin around a lot so she put me in ballet class. So I loved dancing. And that was my invitation to the arts. And then I'm really lucky that my public school had a free theater program. It was very minimalist. It was not fancy. By minimalist, I mean not in a chic way.

SE. The Norwegian meaning, not that.

ET. I think the first play I did was called *Pom-Pom Zombies*. And I played Pandora Spocks, a beatnik hippie. I mean—actually, it was probably the best casting of my life. But we didn't do famous plays. We were within 30 miles of Broadway. So we couldn't do any plays that had been on Broadway in a certain amount of time, because we were within the radius. So we did some really funny shows. So anyway, I started to do theater. I did free theater programs. I got an acting scholarship for this new regional theater that just had been built in Red Bank, New Jersey, called Two River Theater. And it was run by this woman Kate Cordaro (*Director of Education at Two River*), whose name I'll never ever forget. She went to NYU, the Stella Adler program. And so we had these monthly workshops where we learned different theater techniques. We did physical theater and we did Stanislavski and we did clowning and we did mime work and we got free tickets to all the shows. So I started to see theater. I remember I saw…who wrote *Waiting for Godot*?

NA. Beckett.

ET. Yeah, my first Beckett play—no one in my family knows any of this stuff.

SE. Was showing you any of this, yeah.

ET. And I mean, my family still has no idea what I do, or understand it at all—

SE. Same here.

ET. —but they try to be supportive. I love to talk. I love to move. And I think I thought I was gonna do musical theater because I love to sing.

SE. You have a beautiful voice, by the way.

ET. Thank you.

SE. I enjoyed the serenade in *Night Descends on Svalbard*.

ET. Yeah, I loved singing it and that was unplanned. That was us taking a moment of catharsis after—we were just getting these crazy news flashes and were like, "What are we doing?"

SE. "What is happening?"

ET. Making a stupid play in this black box while the world is ending and I'm having, you know, PTSD. I'm like, "Oh my god, my father left Cyprus because a failed coup triggered a war. And now I'm in this theater. And I think there's a coup happening. And now there's going to be a war. Oh, my god!" So anyway—I went to NYU, for theater. I auditioned for two schools: Juilliard and NYU. I got into NYU. It was my dream school. I'm the first woman to go to college in my family. I'm the first artist in my family. My father's the first person to have had a job and not be a literal peasant. Which I think is a funny thing because a lot of times when I say that word in America, people think I'm being condescending. But my family didn't have jobs. They work the land. That's what a peasant is. There wasn't a man that paid them—or a person...

SE. And there's so much honor, in like, being able to cultivate the land and learn from it.

ET. That's why I loved your piece. And that's also why I was thinking about functional art, because I'm always like, "What am I doing?" My grandparents, they know everything about the earth. And really important things, you know? They have first-grade educations. And so I always try to make my work have some sort of function, you know? But a lot of times that function is joy.

SE. Yeah.

ET. Or teaching a lesson or telling a story. In *Night Descends on Svalbard,* part of the function was that Cypriot is an idiolect—for a long time it was called a dialect of Greek, but it's—

SE. How's it called?

ET. Idiolect. A lot of people are advocating for it to be classified as an idiolect, which is different than a dialect. It gives it more power. It's more of an independent language. And—

SE. Oh, so kind of like an idiom-dialect?

ET. Yeah, I think. Greek people can't understand Cypriots

when they talk, but Cypriots can understand Greek people. But I wanted to document the language in my own art. So I spoke Cypriot, specifically, not Greek, because the way that this language gets preserved is if it—

SE. —gets preserved.

ET. —gets preserved, yeah. Not just in a program where I'm like, "Hello, I'd like to record my voice." But to use it in my art. And yeah, we also thought it was really cool to have all different languages like speaking to each other and understanding each other, because I often find that different immigrant groups really do relate to each other more than non-immigrant groups realize.

SE. I think why I keep on going to the gibberish—I think it's so brilliant—because it does destroy this Western hierarchy of languages.

ET. Yeah.

SE. Like, my dad is an engineer and he's got a Master's and whatnot, but my mom, she barely finished elementary school, right? And there's always this idea that you have to speak a language in a certain way to be able to be understood. And when you're an immigrant, there's a whole other pressure of speaking the language correctly and perfectly. And when you put gibberish it's like, "What is language at the end of the day?" Like, we get to make it. To transform it. In the same way that art happens—I mean, "language arts" too, right?

ET. Yeah.

SE. We get to create with them. We get to change them, with

the generations of the communities that keep on working with it. And I think that's something so beautiful, too, about ancestry.

ET. Yeah. Ancestry is something I obviously see in all of your work, and all of the visuals too, and I just love the way that you integrate it into your storytelling. Talking about the darning and the fabric and "this is exactly how it's supposed to be," you know? I was wondering where you learned about the dyes.

SE. The dyes?

ET. Yeah and how to dye the different things.

SE. I feel like I am gonna get very mystical here, but I think a lot of it comes from intuition. And there was something that you were talking about—how your grandparents know the land and how to grow it, and they just naturally went into that. I feel like I learned a lot of cooking from my mom—and a lot of it was intuition. Like, I think she is an amazing cook, her flavors are amazing, and I'm able to replicate, you know, adding certain things here and there, and knowing, "Oh, this works with this. This works with that." And I feel like after being in the kitchen for so long during the pandemic—suddenly my brain started thinking, "Oh, look at that!" Like literally touching things and discovering different colors and pigments and tannins. And when I was walking down the street and seeing the little—like, not the walnuts—what's the—

ET. The acorns?

SE. The acorns! And being like, "Oh my god! I wonder if I boil these things if I'm gonna get something." And I did! And I started doing more research about it. That was something that I always wanted to explore and I never had the time, just because of the hustle and bustle of New York. You're always everywhere—

ET. Yeah.

SE. —not in your kitchen all the time.

ET. The pandemic gave us a lot of time to learn things—that's when I first dyed something with onion skins. Although, I realized this past Easter that for Greek Easter, you dye the eggs red, only red. You don't do a bunch of colors. And I was like, "God. How do I get that deep red?" And they use red onion skins.

SE. Yeah!

ET. I should have known that, but I didn't. But during the pandemic at some point I tried to dye fabric with the red onion skins, and the water was this beautiful fuchsia color but then the fabric was the faintest pink.

SE. It's one of those things when you see the color in the water and then you see it transport into the fabric. You want to see it exactly the same color as the water. But no. It depends on the tannin and the temperature, too. Like once I was dyeing—I think in the video I have all these orange or white onion skins—

ET. Yeah.

SE.—and because of the temperature they turned green! My brain was like, "WHAT!?"

ET. Yeah.

SE. I was like, "That's just life, you know." You try to do something and life throws you whatever is happening and then something else results out of it. It's not bad. It's different. And sometimes really beautiful.

HANNAH KALLENBACH + NICOLÁS NOREÑA

HANNAH KALLENBACH *presented her piece,* 2 Girls, 1 Hotdog, *in the 2018 Exponential Festival, and subsequently returned to the festival with* Wedgie *('19), and with a short film,* Purell Piece *('21). Nicolás Noreña, working with Timothy Scott and their company, The Million Underscores _ _, joined the second Exponential Festival in 2017, presenting their piece,* TELE-VISION: on spiritual displacement. *They followed that up with The Third Man in 2019 and* THOSE MOVEABLE PIECES *in 2024. In addition, Noreña and Scott acted in Object Collection's film,* Look Out Shithead, *as part of the 2021 festival.*

HANNAH KALLENBACH. I was rewatching some footage of your work, and I feel like you're very visual and object-heavy. I'm also visual and object-heavy. I was curious about your process—how you start. It seems like there are so many layers going on. I saw the piece with the paper heads—

NICOLÁS NOREÑA. Oh yeah ... *TELE-VISION: on spiritual displacement.*

HK. Yes! So you have all these different sections that it seems like you built and then paired together in different ways. When you start with your company, is it often that you have this one image in your head of like, "Oh! I see these white paper faces and I want to figure out what that looks like in the space." Do you build it more physically? Or do you just start workshopping writing ideas out? Is it pretty image-based when you start?

NN. Yeah, I mean—I draw.

HK. Okay!

NN. I draw, and a lot of the time I don't really know what I'm doing. Every show is very different, how it starts and how we develop it, and that's an important part of the company; that every show has its own process and its own way of coming together. With *TELE-VISION*, it was interesting because there were five different layers, I think. Because I wanted to make different kinds of programming, kind of like, you know, having—

HK. Like a television.

NN. Yeah. Because my idea was, "What if television wasn't about, like, consumerism, but about, let's say, spiritual displacement?"

HK. Hell yes.

NN. And like, "What would the different programmings be like?" So I was just trying to develop really different performance languages and styles, and working compositionally to put them all together in a space at the same time.

HK. Exciting.

NN. So each one of the sections I worked very differently. With Tim, we were collaborating and co-writing while, with the paper-faced people, there was a lot of improvisation involved. They were drawing spaces that were dear to them, that they didn't have access to anymore. And they would start drawing on the paper that then they would use as masks. Eventually, I choreographed movement from these exploratory improvisations. So, to answer your question: yes, it many times starts from a visual place. And then it's just kind of starting to find different texts and different ideas and different performance languages to work that idea out. How it lives in time...

HK. You're rather choreographic. I was curious if it's built with that performer in the room at the moment, or is it more so in the drawing aspect that you're thinking of this character? When you start putting the objects in the room, is that how characters start coming out?

NN. I mean, I work with performers as the source material. So it's like, I come with a very faint idea into the room. And every time I've been trying to go into rehearsal rooms with less ideas. So that it comes more from my contact with people—so that the origin is really the source material of each person and their energy in the space

HK. Nice! So they're bringing their own character into the image.

NN. Yeah. It's some kind of resonance—a meeting thing.

HK. Yeah, I like that.

NN. I'm also curious how you start finding these really bizarre objects. Like the Mickey Mouse head, or the Purell dispenser, or this thing that I remember you were doing for a while—putting socks on top of shoes. Or over shoes? It seems like your work is very object-oriented and very material. And I'm also curious, how do you begin these relationships with these objects? Is it something that you see on the street, like how we just saw that cabinet? Or is it something that starts calling you at night? What is it?

HK. Yeah, I mean, I think normally I'll see—like how we saw a cabinet outside, and I was like, "Oh, can I fit that in my car?" It was a shattered glass cabinet from a liquor store that had to be moved outside. I was like, "Oh! I could put myself inside of that!" I see something. I was in a bathroom at an airport having a panic attack. Just me in that tiny room, losing my mind—all of a sudden I hear that (*makes mechanical dispenser noise*). And a paper towel dispenser starts shooting out a paper towel. And I just started laughing. I was like, "How dare you interrupt my panic attack!" There was something so personified about it. And I was like, "That's ridiculous. What if the whole bathroom could come to life and give you something that you—a human—needed, without expecting anything in return?" Which automated appliances do. So yeah, it's typically an interaction I have with an object. And then an image of like, "What is the most interesting way my body—or a character or person— might interact with this? And how does that object make me feel? And how do I personify them?" And I saw that there's that great objectum sexual documentary about the woman in love with—

NN. With the bridge?

HK.—and they're married to the Eiffel Tower. And they love their bow, from shooting bows and arrows. There's something so tender about that, and like, theatrical, and perfect, and—it's performance already, just a real-life *need* making its way into unlikely objects and ways that you can get your needs met through many different sources. And so, there's something fun for me in the ability to harness this very vulnerable, raw, kind of scary human emotion without it just being like ...me. So there's some sort of beauty to, "How can we talk about the pain of your dad not speaking to you in a way that I can get people on board at the beginning—where it's comedy, it's light. What can contain this really deep, dark emotion without it just being me having a panic attack on stage?"

NN. Yeah.

HK. Because that's what I *want* to do. Okay, so if I can be Mickey Mouse, Mickey Mouse can talk about their dad (*as Mickey Mouse*) "Hi! It's me, Mickey Mouse! My dad's not talkin' to me. Ha ha!" You know, that's funny. And dark and twisted. And if I leave the rehearsal room going, "Jesus Christ," then I think, "Okay, that's pretty good." Or sometimes it makes me laugh and I'm like, "If I want to see it, then I want to do it."

NN. How do you maintain the freshness of that first encounter with the object? How do you maintain the ridiculousness?

HK. I feel like I really am in love with the thing. If I don't love the idea, it's gonna get abandoned pretty quickly. But if I really like it, I can do it over and over and over again—I mean, it's your acting partner. I have a connection, I guess, to the objects, and to the space that we hold—and there's something about having a scene partner who is giving in a way that doesn't need you to take care of them. In a weird way, that really becomes very (*makes a sorrowful moan*). It hits you while you're looking at the Purell dispenser. It's like, "God! This is so fucking sad." And you're seeing what it is, but also who it could be, or what you need it to be. And I feel like if I love it, if this is something that I enjoy doing, working through something in my life—I think it's all a little drama therapy—then that excites me enough to really hone in…there's like, huge connection there. I really love the objects I work with. And I don't have to pay them! I'm not a solo artist if I get to work with a Purell dispenser. We have fun in rehearsals. I hang out. I wonder if I had the money and funds to have a company if I would be like, "Oh, actually, I love people." Because also what I'm realizing in residencies like being at Mercury Store, is like, "Oh my god, you guys could all be here, and I could pay all of you a living, normal amount and we can collaborate even if I'm working on a solo show. I can have collaborators and I don't have to be alone with a mirror"—and my Purell dispenser, my little sweetie. But yeah, that's what's exciting to me about working with objects. Wait. I was curious, with working at NYU, in the Experimental Theater Wing, and teaching—over time, how has teaching influenced your own artistic process? And maybe vice versa, maybe that's more interesting to you: how your artistic process has influenced you as a teacher?

NN. Well, it's funny because what I teach is something very fundamental to the way that I approach theater, but I kind of have this separation in some way. I mean, not really a separation. What I teach is Mary Overlie's work, so it feels very clean. And I feel very happy doing it. Because I learned how to do it from her. I spent a lot of time with her. So I really learned it like a science, you know, and I can do it.

HK. And you can pass it on.

NN. I can pass it on! Yeah. I'm very proud of that. It's something that I learned how to do. So it's kind of—it's not simple—but I can take this thing that I learned and that I loved and that changed the way that I understood theater, and I can share it with other people. And, on the other hand, my work with The Million Underscores _ _ is very confusing. I usually don't know…I really strive to work from a place of not knowing—and I don't totally fall in love, like you do with objects that carry you forward. It's more a curiosity thing, like, "I have no idea why these things are coming together or why these things are coming into the rehearsal room." And it's just trying to find intricacies. I tend to break things even more so I can understand them less.

HK. When you did the show at Tomato Mouse recently, and it was durational, for many hours, for a few days—

NN. Yes.

HK. —and I pop in on Instagram Live being like "Where's Nico today?" And it's that little security camera looking down and it felt very creepy, but I liked it. Voyeuristic. And I just got to pop in when I wanted to, how I wanted to, without anyone knowing I'm watching, and see you interacting just with the space and with objects and leaving and bringing things in. And I'm curious, after that long amount of time with just you and a bunch of objects, essentially, and experiments that you were trying—like you said, you come in not knowing, and I'm curious what you knew, or didn't know, at the end? What was that like for you?

NN. I mean, it was kind of a traumatizing experience. I still loved it. And I think I'm still digesting it.

HK. It was recent.

NN. It was really intense. It was more intense than I anticipated.

HK. Just the durational aspect?

NN. Yeah. Because it was five days, and it was eight hours. And I thought that I would give myself breaks. I thought, "Oh, I can stop for an hour, leave and go to the hardware store and come back." But then the piece wasn't allowing me to do that. It was just like, "Keep going. You can't have time to think." That's basically how it started going. So it was very tiring.

HK. I'm imagining.

NN. And I was, in a way, completely giving all the energy that I had away.

HK. For eight hours! How do you even—it's a small room.

NN. And then in the back, it was just a giant mess, you know, of wigs and costumes and a bunch of objects. And so I was just going and picking up things. "Where's this wig" and "Where's this costume" and taking a giant tonsil and moving into the space, and suddenly seeing that there's like a person there, or maybe there's no one—I was performing for one person for three hours. It was just one person there in the audience.

HK. They stayed for three hours.

NN. Yeah. And I was feeding (*makes a sucking sound*) like a vampire from this person's energy.

HK. They were feeding from you! Jesus! Three hours?

NN. So I mean, that's what I really started finding in that piece: how much I can feed from the audience. And not even just like, "Oh, they're watching me." But I can take their energy and work with it. Which felt really exciting as a performer and as a theatermaker. Especially with people who I didn't know. This person, I had no idea who this person was. And there were passersby just stopping by and reading the piece, engaging with it, laughing and sitting there.

HK. Yeah, and the moments where you're performing, you feel that energy of another person and then, "Nobody's here…and I am doing *this*?" And you are being recorded, so you know that there are people popping in and out on Instagram Live. What's it like to physically be performing, maybe into the window, but there's no one there?

NN. It's kind of like a nightmare. Because my mom's voice in my head is playing, like, "Why are you doing this?!?" The question is so loud and absolutely paralyzing. But also, after that goes away, there's this very deep feeling of, "Oh, right, this is a strange thing that people have been doing for a long time that nobody can really fully explain. And there's no answer of why we're doing this—we're doing this!" On the last day of the performance I received a bunch of texts of people being like, "Oh, I can't make it today." And I was just (*melting sound*) I just collapsed. You know, I was so incredibly tired from four days of doing it and I was looking forward to having some friends come to see it. When I got to the gallery I went to the backyard, and I was like, "Oh my god. How am I gonna do this?" And then I took a book. I had some books with me there. I took a Clarice Lispector book called *Água Viva*. And with the first page, this woman reached at me through art, you know, being like, "I have no idea how to write this book. And what I'm trying to do is to capture time in its essence, like I want to possess the atoms of time," and I felt company. I thought, "Okay, it's not just about this thing of one person in front of another, but it's this belief that we can send our thinking beyond what we know and send our achievements into very mysterious and deep goals. You know? And that is, in some ways, the role of the artist in society.

HK. Totally. And with performance art, people do durational things that nobody sees, and then, years later, they're like, "For 10 years, I slept on a mattress with bugs." And you're like, "Well, no one fucking saw you do that, but good for you." Like, in hindsight, I will get to look at this creepy video of myself—like, this will be me. I did this. I performed—I did things, for me—I had an experiment that I wanted to try. And I did it. And sometimes there were people and sometimes there wasn't. I find it really interesting as a performer to perform for no one. I mean, half of rehearsals are me and the mirror. And I actually wouldn't be performing, as myself in the mirror, like this, so this is adding a new layer to the fucking show. And then you'll get distracted by your own face and be like, "Oh, God, where was I? I was working. I had a text. Okay, let's face the wall. Face the wall." So that's interesting about performance art. Half of it is just, "I have an experiment I want to try."

NN. Yeah.

HK. "I have no idea what's going to happen and what it means, but it informed my process for something." And then the performance art is, "I did a performance earlier, a long time ago."

NN. I'm curious because I've never been able to think of what I do as performance art. I think about it as theater. But in these moments when we're doing strange experiments, and we find these labels, we take language that gives very different definitions to what we're doing. What is your relationship with the idea of performance art versus theater?

HK. I really go back and forth. Sometimes my bio is like "experimental theater artist." It depends on the piece, though. I mean, I come from a theater background, so I think I just kind of fell into theater hangouts. But experimental theater is so close to performance art. I feel like it's just: are you in a gallery space or are you in a theater?

NN. Yeah.

HK. And who do you know. I know people in the theater. "Can I come in? Can I perform?" But I do think I just got handed that title. I don't feel like I really am, necessarily. It's a weird like, impostor syndrome.

NN. But I think it is true.

HK. Sometimes you're like, "What does this word mean? Am I *it*? Does it depend on the space that I'm in or the type of thing that I'm doing?" Because space really does inform how the audience interacts with it. I think if I did some of the same pieces in MoMA, like in a lobby, that would be performance art somehow. And then if I did it at The Brick, it would be experimental theater, just based on the environment that you're in, the way the audience interacts with it. Can they walk in and out? Is it multiple rooms? But sometimes it's like, "Is it real blood? Or is it fake blood?" If I use my real blood, it's performance art. If I use fake blood, it's experimental theater. I don't know. That's what I thought people were going off of. So I was like, "I guess it is my blood." People are like, "You really did that?" I'm like, "Yeah, but why would I not do the real thing? Why would I get a fake ice sculpture to put in my vagina? I would get a real one."

NN. Right.

HK. Sometimes people say stuff like, "Is it really your mom's birthday?" Why would I say it if it wasn't? I'm like, "Oh. You can lie. You don't have to tell everyone your whole fucking life." That, to me, is why it's performance art in a weird way. Everything I do—I only know this in hindsight—it's all about my childhood and my life. And it's for me. And that's maybe the performance art part, the part that's for me.

KYOUNG PARK + ALEX TATARSKY

In 2018, Kyoung's Pacific Beat presented the play PILLOWTALK *at The Tank in a world premiere with Exponential.* KYOUNG PARK *and his company would go on to present multiple rough-cut screenings of their self-described streamplay,* NERO, *in 2023 and 2024. In addition, Exponential and Kyoung's Pacific Beat were community partners in 2023 and 2024, producing several free community events at the intersection of mutual aid and performance.*

In 2019, ALEX TATARSKY *presented* AMER- ICANA PSYCHOBABBLE (or, my favorite way to die, right now, in this room), *at The Glove.*

ALEX TATARSKY. Just to situate us a bit, could you share the shows you've done at Exponential, and that horrible thing that we have to do all the time, which is, like, a sentence about what they are—

KYOUNG PARK. Oh.

AT. —and yeah, how you identify in relation to theater? Like, is there a role that you call yourself?

KP. So, for Exponential, we've worked on two pieces. In 2018, we premiered a show called *PILLOWTALK,* a gay bedroom drama between an Asian-American and African-American man, whose sort of Long Day's Journey into *that* Night becomes about race and class and internalized racism and homophobia, and how, throughout that piece, those things become expressions of a pas de deux through which they liberate themselves from that internalized oppression. It's kind of like a love story turned into ballet. And the second piece, *NERO*, it's a much longer epic, about George W. Bush's War on Terror that we retell as the story of the rise and fall of Nero's Roman Empire. And because of the pandemic, this very big Shakespearean epic has become a five-part miniseries that we shot as a film project. I guess for both of those pieces, I'm the writer and the director. But I am a trained writer. I'm a self-taught everything else. How about you?

AT. Yeah, I did a piece called *AMERICANA PSYCHOBAB-BLE* at The Glove—R.I.P. It was for Exponential in 2019. And that piece is sort of exercising and exorcising some demons of the American psyche. Really going into different states and seeing what kind of associative language burbled up. The main throughline is inspired by a photograph of fingernails that are painted with the American flag, and thinking, "What would these fingernails say if they could speak?" Really trying to release some language in a non-linear, non-narrative way that spoke to the monstrosity of what's lurking underneath the red, white, and blue. And trying to channel the specific textural qualities of the American flag fingernails, their brittleness and shininess. In this photograph are what, to me, looked like white female hands kind of clawing and grasping. So just letting the language emerge from that image of a body part and a flag. I identify as a clown. So that's my practice.

KP. Watching *AMERICANA PSYCHOBABBLE*, I did see how your practice in clowning, Lecoq, and buffoonery showed up. And I saw you as a performer becoming almost taken over by the voices of MAGA and Trumpism. And throughout that performance, it felt like this healing exorcism where you're trying to get rid of white supremacy through this very funny ritualistic suicide with a hotdog, and then like ruminating musically as an Angel of Death. I'm glad you brought up this picture, because I was curious about what came first: was it the embodiment? Was it an image? Was it the language? I was also wondering about the babbling and the psychobabble, just because so much of the language felt like—you know pataphysics?—like you could say one thing and it could mean like eight different things depending on how you say it, who's saying it, and who you're saying it to. Could you speak about that relationship, the translating of images into words?

AT. It definitely came out of an improvisational practice that felt very much like spirit-channeling. Or another way that I would put it is channel surfing, tuning yourself to a particular frequency, and seeing what comes through. And specifically thinking about language sculpturally and breaking it into bits and seeing what emerges from that mode of breaking down. The sonic leaps of logic and sense-making. I began the practice around 2016, not explicitly about Trump, who wasn't president yet, but I think in some way responding to the feeling of political discourse in that moment, which had such a strong nonsense bent like, it really seemed like everyone was speaking nonsense. And as a nonsense practitioner, and a person who's really devoted to traditions of poetic nonsense, I felt kind of nervous and upset, like, "I must take nonsense back from the claws of those who are misusing it or using it for really quite evil ends." It's like, I want to defend nonsense as something that can be world-building in a really beautiful way by shifting how we think and see and communicate, not something that is so destructive and causing so much confusion and the inability for anyone to speak to each other. That makes me want to ask how you're thinking about language and registers in your own work, because I was really struck by the humor in *PILLOWTALK* and the quality of the dialogue. Since I'm a solo performer, primarily, dialogue is really intriguing and impressive to me. My dialogue feels like it's with the audience, and you're creating these conversations between the characters that are dealing with such heavy topics, but there's often such humor and a kind of self-deprecation. One question is, in what way do you feel like you are speaking through the characters? Like what is your relationship to what you're having them say? I'm also really curious about how humor is operating, and the ways in which the characters reflect on themselves or seem to wink at the audience a bit.

KP. With *PILLOWTALK* in particular, I had written it for two actors and one of them was Daniel Isaac, who had done two shows with us before. And he is an incredibly comedic actor. So I knew that I wanted to write something funny for him. And he had asked me that we do a very normal show. So the most normal thing I could conceive of was just two characters having a conversation in a bedroom. I was writing from my personal experiences—Daniel is a queer Korean actor whose Korean name is also Kyoung, and was my foil—and the counterpoint became my husband, Daniel Lim. We met doing community work where the intersections of race and sexual orientation were what brought us together. So having that kind of conversation between the characters became very easy for me, because that's the kind of intersectionality that was bringing the people I cared about together in a loving kind of space. But I think the thing with making dialogue theatrical—from a playwright's point of view—is that you don't want to be preachy or pat people on the back by just affirming what we believe. So there was this desire to constantly flip what the characters were saying and try to push the conversations past the point of logic, so that we weren't affirming our assumptions, but rather, digging deeper into what feels very structural and invisible in the ways we relate to each other as humans, and finding the deeper roots of where a disconnect or oppression comes from. So the only way to do that was to push the logic of the dialogue to the point of absurdity, because that's usually where the logic broke and something else was found. That's also where we found the humor because usually, that breaking point was the funny.

AT. The play opens with a reflection on the doom-ness of writing in relation to one's political ideals and desires, what an individual and what an artist can accomplish. I was like, "Oh, this is really intriguing to see a piece that's, in a very light-handed way, making a metacommentary on art-making and on writing from the very beginning, in terms of confronting what it can ever really do to change the world." So I'm curious how you grapple with...

KP. Like, how futile is it?

AT. Yeah, like, what do you understand the aim of a play to be, for instance?

KP. Yeah.

AT. Horrible question, by the way.

KP. No, I mean, I get it. It's totally ridiculous, right? Like, there's no point in playwriting. You won't make a living out of it. We started a peacemaking theater company—what the hell is that? There are so many utopian values in the work of our company, but I also think that there's no pragmatic sense to it at all. You know, it's completely futile. But it's who I am. And it's an authentic expression of myself. And when you're legible in so many other ways, because of your race, or your gender, or your nationality status, for me to be able to say, "I am a peacemaking theater artist"—the empowerment of saying: "That is actually the truest expression of myself as an artist," it's why I keep doing it. And I don't think that everyone in our company identifies the same way. I think I work with a lot of people who really believe in me and want to support me, in that sense, as an artist. And usually, that's how I find the collaborators I find. We're not doing it because we're all Asian, or we're all fighting for the same kind of queer rights, you know? There's something more honest, I think, about doing something even though it makes no logical sense. That makes me think of my question for you. So this week, I saw Dmitry Krymov's *Big Trip* at La MaMa. And I'm still very thoughtful, seeing a Russian artist who has chosen to self-exile and respond to Russia's war in Ukraine through his pieces, which really rely heavily on clowning to make the truth go down with laughter. And as I was watching those pieces, it made me think of the distance we need as artists to the societal problems we're making work in response to. You know, what is the distance that we need as artists and healers to function? Because sometimes, we're just outcast, or called in when needed to do what we do, you know? So now, this year being 2023, I'm wondering: who is in your company, in the peripheries? And who are you staying away from these days?

AT. Wooo...fascinating question. Well, right before I came here, I was at a community garden in Loisaida called De Colores. And I saw a bunch of poetry and music organized by my personal guru, this poet, Sparrow, who I'm just continually smitten with. He is wandering around the garden barefoot in a fur coat and a baseball cap that says, like, "Ford Motor Company" pulled down really low. He has a long, long, long gray beard. And he has this band called Truffles. The instruments that Sparrow plays are, like, dropping two plastic spoons onto a Tupperware. Or like, rearranging some leaves. And it's just so hilarious and so heartbreaking and so tender and poignant, and incisive, in a way—maybe in response to some of these things you were talking about—like, the obvious futility of what we do alongside its necessity. It gives me so much hope and joy to see that kind of performance where I feel energetically rearranged by being there, and being with other people in the shared present moment. And at one point Sparrow made everybody do a wiggle dance and I tend to really hate being told what to do as an audience member—even though I generally do this to my audience so I have to think about that more—but just the mere act of wiggling...If I had to answer your question, it's like: who are the people who believe in "wiggling"? Who believe in trying to find a way to be present in our particular physical containers with each other? Who believe in what movement can do to physically rearrange our molecules, rearrange how we're thinking and feeling together? Lisa Fagan is someone who comes to mind who's also been an Exponential artist where, like, I'm in the presence of her relationship to movement and absurdity, and deconstructing narrative, and I'm just like—

KP. And she's hysterical.

AT. And she's hysterical. Her work makes me think differently somehow, even though it would be hard to articulate how, which is delightful. Because then you get to keep chewing on it, like, "Why is this making sense? It's not making sense. But it is making sense."

KP. It's making nonsense!

AT. It's making nonsense so *well*!

KP. Oh, and then, who do you feel like you're staying away from?

AT. I knew there was a part of the question I was avoiding but I couldn't remember what it was. You mean, like, what kind of work?

KP. I meant more like...for example, after 2020, I went through this moment of being like: I'll see how many white friends I have left after this pandemic is over. And it's not to generalize white people, it's just that something shifted, you know? I found community in my neighborhood, I found community in just figuring out how to relate to those I actually care about in a city of millions, and to really deepen those relationships. I've made choices in this return to whatever this is. I hear you talking about the artists and the spaces, the natural spaces, you want to be present in. Where do you find yourself not present?

AT. The whole period around 2020, when theaters shut down really revealed to me that we don't need institutions, but we think we do. And that institutions, as we know, mostly serve to perpetuate themselves, and are really entrenched in a lot of these things we're talking about, in white supremacy and how it functions to exclude, and to exploit, and to extract, and to exhaust. It's been pretty painful returning to "normal." I was really curious, actually, about the moment in your play where the performer requests a "normal play." We no longer say "back to normal" so much, but that phrase was floating around for a while, like, "When are things gonna get back to normal?" I'm really trying to grapple with being excited by the possibility of making some kind of a living as a performer while also really feeling strongly in my body that institutions, no matter how radical they claim to be, tend to take the things that we make and neuter them. Or say that they're making radical changes but structurally everything stays exactly the same and is perhaps even obscured by the radical rhetoric in some way.

KP. Yeah, I hear you.

NA. Speaking of institutions.

(*Nic gives the 5-minute warning.*)

KP. I just want to say how much I relate to this questioning of the future of our institutions. And, you know, the rhetorics that you've shared. For me, I consider that we have survived terrible times and have found ways to make it through without those institutions, so the ways we have succeeded are the indicators of what's possible, you know? I'm not interested in leaving this space or leaving this energy behind, but just kind of staying with it as my new normal.

And it's very different. It feels like an alternative space you've built and want to invite other people to come join you. Last question: in one of your interviews you mentioned Goethe's *Wilhelm Meister's Theatrical Mission* as an ongoing, lifelong performance you're envisioning. And I kind of saw that almost as an arc to your own journey as a performance artist. So I'm wondering, not knowing what this reference is, how *AMERICANA PSYCHOBABBLE* and your next show, *Sad Boys in Harpy Land*, kind of fit in that journey?

AT. *Wilhelm Meister's Theatrical Mission,* as a project, started before *PSYCHOBABBLE.* I started working on it in 2014, at La MaMa, E.T.C. when I discovered this really long novel by Goethe that follows a small German boy who wants to be a theater artist, and his various struggles with that desire. And it was so resonant with what I felt in myself and what I saw in a lot of my peers that I was kind of horrified. I had the sensation of being trapped in a narrative. Have we become trapped in the same narrative? This book was written in 1795! But many of the issues have stayed the same: in particular the relationship between the theater and the state, and ongoing considerations of the role of theater as a didactic tool to shape people and to teach people how to be in the world. And what is the responsibility of the artist in relation to that task? How can you trouble the expectation implicit in that task when you still need funding from somewhere? This has always been the problem of theater artists, especially, because you need space. Jack Smith—who's another one of my heroes—says that at the heart of every play are the evils of landlordism because the playwright is always dealing with the person who owns the land on which the theater sits. So in some way, every play has to grapple with that power dynamic. Like how do you say the things you want to say while not getting evicted? Shakespeare's Globe Theater was built on leased land, right? Seeing Goethe grapple with some of these dynamics was so fascinating to me. I couldn't let go of feeling like I was identifying with Wilhelm Meister. This is 1795, the Prussian empire is expanding its territory, and Wilhelm's father has had some success in business. So Wilhelm is able to sit around and contemplate these questions of the theater because he comes from a privileged family. And that creates a kind of despicable, very present tension, that I feel in myself and a lot of my peers that often goes unacknowledged. Like, who has—

KP. The privilege.

AT. —the privilege to sit around and really think about the role of theater in the world? I was like, "Oh, my God! I'm Wilhelm! I'm gonna kill myself." Like, I don't want to be Wilhelm. And then the dynamics of our own particular entangled histories as, like, a diasporic Jew identifying with these German theorists and theater-makers. And of course, there's all this racism embedded in the narrative. Like, Wilhelm loves going to watch the Black minstrels that come through town. And he loves pretending to be a Jew as a funny caricature. He's unable to grapple with his whiteness and privilege, and these same issues of theater and appropriation filter through this book from the 1700s. I'm trying to untangle the category or creation of whiteness as it comes into being by performing the other. Which brings me finally to your interest in empire through the figure of Nero. How did you come to Nero as a framing for that work? How do you grapple with your relationship to power in this moment of collapse of empire?

KP. So this is maybe my fourth or fifth 9/11 play. I came of age as a young artist during those days—like, I woke up to the second plane crashing into the Twin Towers. I was in Chinatown and that woke me up that morning. The anti-war movement, the War on Terror and its consequences have been subjects I've researched and written about for maybe 20 years. But this is my last play about it. I'm so done with it, you know? But the war didn't really end until the time we were workshopping NERO in '22. This war has been an ongoing source of tension, and source of violence, for so much of my adult life. It was very hard to pretend like it wasn't happening because it was ongoing all this time. For NERO, I wanted to write from the point of view of the people who were making decisions about this war. I've written plays about the protests, or the experience living through 9/11 in New York, and you know, essays based on interviews of people who lost loved ones in the planes or in the Twin Towers, but I just really wanted to get into the minds of the psychopaths who decided to have this war. That's what NERO is for me. And you know, the founder of Peace Studies, Johan Galtung, predicted that this war will lead to the "fall of the American Empire." Like, he saw the American Empire rise since World War II, and kind of foresaw its collapse by 2025 based on the histories of previous wars and Empires. I wanted to dramatize that. And I think, you know, sort of similar to you, I've been asking myself. "Why are we stuck in narratives?" As a young artist, I wanted to be a tragedian. In school, they said: "There were the Greeks, then there was Shakespeare, maybe Ibsen, and no one else." And I was like: "I'm gonna be the one after Ibsen!" You know? Like, that was my obsession. I wanted to write tragedies. And everything I've written has had that form. But Boal's *Theater of the Oppressed* just obliterated that obsession, because he wrote about how that form was created to oppress the public consciousness and to make us like, not be extraordinary. Because we're watching the downfall of all these great people in front of us, to remind us that we should not dare to, you know? So *NERO* is, for me, the last of my tragic plays. I'm so done with tragedy anyway. I'm so tired of this futility we talk about. The tragedy of the daily news. I'm so tired of this pointlessness, you know?

ANN MARIE DORR + KATE KREMER

KATE KREMER's Term of Art *and Ann Marie Dorr's collaborative performance with Paul Ketchum,* Good and Noble Beings, *were presented in the 2020 Exponential Festival.*

KATE KREMER. I'm curious about how being a producer of others' work has changed your relationship to making your own work. Especially in a moment when you're maybe transitioning away from producing?

ANN MARIE DORR. Well, I think *Good and Noble Beings* was me really starting to commit to the idea that I could make work. And not just like, supporting or facilitating other people's work. It was happening at a time when I worked at The Bushwick Starr as a production manager, and during the course of the Soho Rep Writer Director Lab, Paul and I started the project for real. I then left The Bushwick Starr at the end of 2018, so by the time we were at Exponential, I was really starting to free myself from being like, "Oh, this is what I do for money." Or, I feel like I spent 10 years learning how to make work from other people by changing their work, and a lot of new plays and new devised pieces. And so I think I've picked up all these different tools, especially about how writers function in the room, or sometimes decide to exclude themselves from a room. Which I think is sort of a different—is a generational thing?

KK. Like an older generation tends to be less present in the room, would you say?

AMD. Not always. Like, some people are just "Here, I'm handing you the play. And, we'll talk about edits, and I'll bring in pages." Or, "This play is really done. And I don't want to do edits." Which are all valid things. But I've always found myself to be happier in rooms where people are all in it. And changing it. And making it, I don't know, "better." So I think that drive also filters into my work. Paul and I have done four public iterations of *Good and Noble* and we make a lot of jokes about how this piece we could do for the rest of our lives, because of the decision to bring our personal lives into it. Which is also part of my journey as a maker, is sort of being like, "Oh, I'm gonna bring myself to the table." In fact, during 2020, we were on a Zoom with Theresa Buchheister, and we made a joke about doing *Good and Noble* in 2050. And so in some Google calendar somewhere, there is an event for *Good and Noble* in 2050. So we'll see.

KK. Love it.

AMD. Maybe we'll just have holograms—many, many Kedians (*collaborator Kedian Keohan*) in very different forms. But yeah, I think my sensibility is sort of this big patchwork of working with lots of—a lot of different playwrights, actually, who've gone to Brooklyn College, and a lot of different makers within the downtown experimental lineage.

KK. To come in as both as a producer and a person with production management experience—you are so familiar with the physical infrastructural tools of theater-making, like the pragmatics of it, which really animates *Good and Noble Beings*. I feel like that project is thrumming with the awareness of the different things a show can do. And the different ways it can inhabit a space, the different ways you can layer things on top of each other, the different ways media can be incorporated. It feels like a show that is using tools. Not in a—not in a flashy way, but in a casual, "These were in my bag" kind of way.

AMD. Yeah, it's very analog. I'm much more attracted to that aesthetic of analog tools. I mean, we are using video, but in like the most basic of ways that we can, I think. Recording videos of Kedian doing the text with a silly little GoPro that I have or with our phones has always sort of been the aesthetic in that realm. Using old computer monitors, instead of lots of different built video-surface stuff.

KK. One of the things I was gonna ask about is the use of "memoir," or writing in an auto-fictive mode, which I think is a strategy we share. I'm thinking about the way that can bring in a casualness or a personal quality—the texture of the real in the room. And then I'm also thinking about errors and failure. And I guess maybe the relationship between those three things: errors and failure and the self.

AMD. Oh, I think Paul and I are obsessed with all of those things. I mean, I feel constantly on a journey with failure, and not in a negative connotation. I think the willingness for something to not work is an interesting space to live in. I'm curious how that has worked for you.

KK. I think in *Term of Art*, one of the strategies that I had for incorporating failure in a nightly, physical way was having the transcriptionist on stage. Having a person who was there, trying to write down everything they heard, which is not possible. I mean, people talk fast, hands write slowly. And then hearing that transcript in the middle part of the show was a way of framing the aporias and the absences—registering the holes in our transcript was a way of thinking about all the holes and the errors and smudges in the official record. The Supreme Court transcripts that I was looking at are of course also quirkily riddled with errors and blanks—the way that people actually speak—and they're also riddled with logical holes or breakages and slides, kind of intentional occlusions that allow a person to make one kind of argument rather than another. And so I think *Term of Art* ended up being very much about that question of how a particular argument gets framed, how a particular line gets drawn. I was just listening on the radio to some new study about how we're not gonna be able to stop global warming at 1.5 degrees Celsius. And on NPR, they were doing all this work to be like, "We're not going to stop it, it's gonna be higher than 1.5 degrees Celsius, but 1.5 isn't a *cliff*! We're not dropping off a *cliff*! Don't everybody just quit!" And *Term of Art* is thinking about the way that the border gets narrativized as being something that's so firm and so rigid. And actually, it's always a gradation, if it exists at all. Like the border between childhood and adulthood—a 17-year-old and an 18-year-old are totally the same. And yet, legally, they're different. You know, the US and Mexico have—that border is entirely constructed, but also enforced.

AMD. Yeah, I think there's something in that gradation or in exploring rhizomatic, nonhierarchical making, that is related to the concept of borders.

KK. Oh yeah, the borders are a way that we're striating space. I was so interested in the metaphors that you guys use to illustrate rhizomes, I mean, like the wasp and the orchid. But I was also thinking about the way that *Good and Noble*

Beings has itself such a rhizomatic structure—like the way that Paul lays out some of the terminology at the beginning—and then, during the rest of the play I was thinking back to that terminology and making connections to the stories people were telling. Like the idea of the beginning of a relationship being a smooth space because there are no habits. And then I was like, well, "Is Tinder a smooth space?" But it so clearly, quickly, isn't, you know? And so with each of those vignettes, I felt the impulse as an audience member to draw connections. And at the same time, there are multiple visual things that are happening, that I'm also trying to piece together. Like Kedian taping the floor. So I thought about that rhizomatic structure—to what degree can you hold onto the smoothness of this space, to a lack of hierarchy, and to what degree, as soon as two people are speaking, like when you start speaking over Paul, how all I'm immediately listening to is you? Do you know what I mean? That there's immediately a hierarchy that my ear makes. Or maybe it's that you are speaking with a microphone, but like, yeah, my attention isn't egalitarian.

AMD. Yeah, letting an audience watch a thing and draw their own lines is really, was always very exciting for us. How do we give people enough information to build from and not just feel like they're being told what the piece is? I've watched it a few times since we've done it. But I'd be curious to watch it again and think about that more. Ultimately, Paul and I realized, "Oh, there's no way for us to avoid hierarchy in our making." But we can try our darndest to at least have everybody who's participating in the room—I think even, hopefully, the audience—to have their own path. But doing it 9 or 10 times in a row—at what point do we ask while performing, "When are we going to make different decisions with the information that we have?" Also, what are the different decisions that Jeff Aaron Bryant is gonna make as the person who is sort of in charge of the video/sound world. Like Jeff's sort of in his own world, and isn't—and has his moments of taking over the hierarchy that I still have like a desire to explore more, like what Jeff's presence/non-presence is. It's also interesting in your piece. Sound, in particular, as this compositional layer, and how it does inform us. My relationship to that has shifted since working on the piece though, through working with d/Deaf/hard-of-hearing and disabled artists and learning more about access. So I am thinking about this piece now that I am more informed about access practices—

KK. How will thinking about accessibility will change your making, either in production or in terms of the writing?

AMD. I've had a little bit of conversation with an access dramaturg friend, about how live-transcribing and captioning—would really fit into the world. I've been thinking a lot about how, if access isn't built in from the beginning, do we integrate it? And how do we integrate access into the aesthetic that we already have? I haven't totally wrapped my brain around how audio description would work in the piece. But I think that having live transcription—as you were saying before, hands work at a different speed than our mouths and our ears and our senses in general. And so how does that inform a hierarchy in the room? We're also slightly more trained—I mean, I feel like a lot of people watch everything with captions on now, and so we're a more trained audience for that. Like access has benefited all people in that way

KK. Yeah. Well, I was thinking about that moment where Kedian is speaking and then there's the live-captioning of Kedian's speech. I really liked that moment because the caption is so riddled with errors, and how that felt like that was speaking to the concerns of the piece. Of failure, of the recognition, the "recognition on top of recognition," is that the phrase? Like, are you also going to burn the cookies? And the fact that there were so many different kinds of sensory experiences happening in your piece, like, there must have been a smell of baking cookies. So there's something about the autonomy of each person choosing at any moment what to pay attention to. And giving performers and designers that same kind of autonomy feels dynamic and yeah, as egalitarian as it gets.

AMD. I think if we were really to commit to doing it again, I have a bigger, more expansive thought around our autonomy—how is all of our autonomy leading to, or failing at leading to, collective autonomy? And I'm pretty over the individualism that I experience or feel in theater, in the world, in general—how am I making work that is more about the collective?

KK. And what are the opportunities for autonomy within the collective? Like, what are the dynamics of sharing? Of collectivity, of coming together? And then also, what are the dynamics within that collectivity of dissonance and dissent and autonomous choice-making? And also, how do we prepare ourselves for the inevitable occasional failures that are going to happen in that model of collectivity?

AMD. We both did shows in 2020, and like, how do you feel about your piece and how has it evolved for you with time?

KK. Yeah, I mean, the issues or the questions of the piece have remained really pressing. I think I imagined at the time of making it that it was going to be something we would continue to perform in other contexts. And that has felt really impossible and distant. I haven't felt like making theater makes sense to me at all, in my life or in the broader ecosystem, the broader political ecosystem. So, I don't know. I'm finally starting to think about what would it mean to put something on stage. I'm still thinking about the tools we were using in *Term of Art*, like the disjunction of movement and text. Certainly, I'm still collaging, though it's a different kind of practice. So yeah. It feels very far away. But I still want those ideas to be in the world.

AMD. Yeah. That is the thing about theater, or the culture. We want to do things again, and when is it okay to just be like, "That thing happened. And it doesn't have to happen again. But what can I take from it and continue to build that feels valuable to me right now in the ecosystem?"

NIC ADAMS + MARISSA JOYCE STAMPS

NIC ADAMS *is the Producing Director of The Exponential Festival. He joined the festival's curation and administrative team in 2017. As an artist, Adams presented work with Exponential in 2017 with* Icarus in the L.E.S., *in 2019 with* Duet-ed, *created with Cori Marquis, in 2021 with* "Stiff Drink!?" *with Dr. Eustice Sissy (Psy.D.), presents:* "Corona Cam Show" *with Lee Rayment, and in 2025 with* Rainbow's End, *directed by Marissa Joyce Stamps.*

MARISSA JOYCE STAMPS *was part of the 2022 Exponential Festival, presenting her play,* Blue Fire Burns the Hottest. *In 2024, she returned to Exponential with* Being Up in Here and All the Other Businesses that Don't Concern You OR When You See a Buncha Black People Running, What Do You Do? *(hereafter* Being Up in Here...*)*

NIC ADAMS. More and more when I see productions, what excites me is the idea of unique group play; watching a company—performers, writer, director, designers, crew maybe—who have a really deep shared performance vocabulary—

MARISSA JOYCE STAMPS. Yeah, yeah.

NA. And upon watching the video you sent me for *untitled water piece*, and thinking about the other plays of yours I know, I thought, "Marissa's unique group play incorporates storytelling, the occupation of and movement within large amounts of space, a healthy balance between silence and speaking, and focuses on duos, trios, and groups, instead of individual protagonists."

MJS. That feels right.

NA. How much of that is intuitive? How much of that is intentional? And why those things?

MJS. I was doing the lil' granty-grant thing the other day, and I was like, "Dang, I gotta, like, add something new, right? So they know I'm not just reusing my artistic statement." So I was like, "Okay, what is something that I've discovered in the past three years about my work?" And I think you're right on that I think in terms of the duo, trio group play instead of the protagonist. I think in my mind's eye, there's always a protagonist, but I'm less interested in centering on that character for an extended period of time because, for me, we're always in this sort of exchange of energy with people. Whether that be like, spiritually, energetically, emotionally, or physically. So I try to think of nuanced ways to put that on stage. I think what also is helpful is I usually start writing from a place of love.

(The interview gets interrupted.)

MJS. (*Reviewing for herself*) Duos, trios, shared energy that is within the environment. That's the container for the piece. I think a lot about that. It's looking to environment and landscape as the character and using that to see: how do the energies between these people flow? So for *Blue Fire* I was like, "Even though we have this duo—what are the containers they can exist in? Like, this is the boxing ring.

Like, here's a square that can contain the fighting energy. And then the inner square is where we revisit the past, which is also a different type of duel but more so like an emotional duel.

NA. Right.

MJS. And then, how are their egos shifted in and out of the ring? So I think about landscape like that. Also environmental landscape outside of artificial, manmade spaces. Yeah—

NA. I'm thinking about the tub.

MJS. Yeah!

NA. The tub is not "realistic" in terms of its proximity to the boxing ring, but is emotionally very real.

MJS. It's like—the tub was the first image that came to mind when I started writing *Blue Fire*. For me, that space is like the container for self-reflection, looking at baptism, cleansing, the place where they can be or *attempt to be* their most authentic selves and are the most connected to their spirituality.

NA. So many of the landscapes in your plays have stuck with me. The hotel from *Vètij*, the swamp from *Letiche*...the roll, skate, walkathon?

MJS. *Walk-Bike-Skate-a-Thon*. There you go.

NA. Yeah. And then this piece, *untitled water piece*, where you have these great speeches about, like, overhearing things across a lake—

MJS. Oh, my gosh, so that was Yansa Fatima, one of the

actors at Mercury Store, and how that came about was it was me, Yansa, our intimacy director, jo Valdés, and then our stage manager, Gia Ramos. And I just told Yansa to, like, go back to a memory that they had shared. I wish I had written that because that was amazing. Basically, we started the week off with sort of, like, an inverted outline, where we didn't really have any outline, per se, and then by the end, I was like, "Okay, this is our container." But a lot of our discussion with the group of eight actors was looking at our relationship to water as Black women and femmes and—"Do we have a good relationship with water? Do we not?" Like, water in artificial spaces versus natural spaces. And so Yansa was actually—if I'm remembering correctly—Yansa was *not* a fan of water, but appreciated being—like just observing in those spaces but not being submerged in it. So that's—that's where that story came from. And—

NA. But it was your idea to put characters in proximity to that landscape.

MJS. Yeah, yeah, yeah. 100%. Yeah. I feel the most myself as a human being in nature. And I'm always just like, trying to find ways to make it a character in plays.

NA. That's a consistently moving aspect of your work—the location and its presence. Thinking of location, and space, and movement, and the Mercury Store residency and *deadbodydeadbodydeadbody*—something that interests me is you come directly out of NYU undergrad actor training into the Brooklyn College grad program for playwriting, where we met. My question is, do you think of yourself as a playwright?

MJS. I do think of myself as a playwright! I think—

NA. Is that important to you?

MJS. Hm…"Is it important to me?" Can you clarify what you mean by that?

NA. To me, your work is so much about embodiment and groups. And I look at your work and I'm like, "Wow, Marissa can choreograph! Marissa can write! Marissa can direct!" Another way of asking that question is, when you decided to go to Brooklyn College to study playwriting, what was that experiment about?

MJS. The experiment of going to Brooklyn College? If I'm gonna be completely honest, the experiment of going to Brooklyn College was like—I know I'm a playwright—like 2021, playwright graduating from NYU—if you are going to take me seriously as a Black woman, I gotta get this MFA.

NA. Yeah.

MJS. So that was the experiment. And I think like, with that experiment, there was a lot of, "Here's what I'm learning from other playwrights about their practice, and what I could borrow." Like things that maybe I don't like, but now I know that I don't like them. Because like, 2020-2021 was the first year I really took myself seriously as a playwright or saw it as a career. Because, we were all in solitude, so I guess I was like, "I'll just write. I guess I'll finish this play." I had always wanted to go to grad school. And I just thought that now was a good time. And in terms of like—everyone is sitting in stillness. Like, the worst thing they can say is "No." And they said "Yes." I guess the reason I asked to clarify was because recently I've been thinking a lot about recognition and success. And this has come up in *Being Up in Here* rehearsals where it's like, looking for validation that you're living in your purpose. And whether that comes from outside sources or yourself. Or you think something is your purpose, and then like, what your soul is actually saying to you. So I think what's come up, like, literally within the past two weeks of being in this rehearsal room, is that I think it's important that I know I'm a playwright for myself. And I also think it's dangerous, for me, if that's the only thing that I can identify with, without recognizing things that I'm not only just *good* at but things that bring me *joy* that I might *not* be good at, you know?

NA. Uh huh.

MJS. I just think that knowing what you're doing and *the why* is important. And it's always good to reevaluate. That was a tangent, but I've been thinking a lot about, like, success.

NA. When I was reading your scripts in class, I was often thinking, "This is going to blow up in performance. There are things that Marissa can invent with bodies that she is not putting in this script right now." And that excited me so much. I also identify with you in this sense. You produce your plays, you market your plays, you direct them, and choreograph them, you regard so much of the production as an extension of the storytelling. You involve yourself and put artistry into the marketing graphic, or the scene that is in silence, and, in contrast, I've noticed that there's a trend where people are like, "Oh, I only have one artistic practice: I direct." And there's a part of me that's intimidated by that focus and specialization, because I want to keep doing a lot of different things, artistically.

MJS. Yeah, I was just going to ask you: when did you figure out that you were a multi-disciplinary artist?

NA. From the minute I could walk? I mean, early artistic memories for me: I would go and see my dad play in his surf rock band and I would dance as part of the crowd.

MJS. Nic is a dancer first.

NA. I grew up dancing. I would book time in first grade to debut new dances at the end of class. Most of my routines were set to Michael Jackson songs, one was to a song from *Oliver & Company*.

MJS. *Oliver & Company*!

NA. So dancing was early. Playing the drums was early. My dad's a musician so as soon as I had motor skills, he was like—

MJS. "Here ya go!"

NA.—"Learn how to play an instrument." And I was obsessed with Michael Jackson. And he could sing *and* dance, right?

MJS. Yes he could.

NA. And so my role models were artists who did a couple of things, at least. I believed that's what it meant to be an artist. And writing songs was something I was doing early on. I wrote a pastiche of Michael Jackson's "Thriller" called "Terror Town," which had the—

MJS. (*Chuckling*) "Terror Town" ...

NA.—same meter, the same melody as "Thriller," but it was just different words.

(*Marissa hums the bassline.*)

NA. Yeah, exactly. It wasn't until I got to college that I met people who were so confidently, like, "I am *only* an actor." Like it was a fixed, singular identity. And I couldn't relate. It kind of freaked me out. I wondered how these people were so certain that they were gonna do just this one thing.

MJS. Right. You're like 18.

NA. So it started really young, doing multiple artistic things, and then it grew into this…but I mostly applied my other interests *to* theater. Even if I was writing a song, it would be a song for a play.

MJS. Right.

NA. And if I was producing, I was producing a live event that was going to be performed. Which makes me think…there is often a point when you're self-producing where it's like, "Welp, we ran out of money, and we can't actually hire a stage manager. I guess I will stage manage this show that I've also written and also directed and also designed." I don't know if that's necessarily a bad thing—

MJS. No, it's not a bad thing.

NA. What's your take on it?

MJS. My take is, we just need more resources.

NA. Yeah.

MJS. But I totally relate, I mean, during *Blue Fire* I was like, "If one of y'all gets sick, I have to go in. I pray that I don't," and like—you write the play for a year, you direct it, you know it—I like knew the lines but like, "Damn, I haven't acted in a long time."

NA. Right.

MJS. "But I gotta go in!"

NA. Right!

MJS. Because COVID was, you know—

NA. You postponed from Omicron—you were supposed to do the show in January of 2022.

MJS. That's correct. And then we had to wait those nine months and do it in September. And that's why we did *deadbodydeadbodydeadbody* in the middle.

NA. Yeah.

MJS. Because I was like, "The momentum is too good to not do something." Like, "We gotta keep the public interest and we got to make it seem like (*actors*) Moses Chavez-Gray and Danté Charles Crichlow are about to have a fight."

NA. You totally created that energy and that buzz and that story. When I watched *deadbody*, I thought, "I'm having my first course before I have the main"—

MJS. Yeah, that was a special meal. Like, *deadbody* was a one-night thing. You see it and you have more context going into this play, or just go into *Blue Fire*.

NA. Changing topics. You wrote on your website for *a dias-*

pora in self-isolation, "The difference between proof and documentation is this: to 'prove something' means that there is the chance that there is something that might not be real. To 'document something' means that you are simply recording what is real and what is actually happening." You're getting well-deserved recognition for your work right now. And it's really exciting to watch. In thinking about opportunities like a commission, a writers' group, etc., do you have a pretty good gut instinct about when people are asking you to "prove" yourself and when people are asking you to "document" yourself?

MJS. I feel like in terms of documenting myself, it's just me being me.

NA. Yeah.

MJS. Like, I am "the document." And it's like, I am either going to be held in this space or not. That is how I know that you trust the documentation. Whereas, the proof is like—listen, I'm gonna have the documentation—I got the recordings.

NA. You've got the receipts.

MJS. I've got the receipts! I think a lot of times I'm asked to, like, prove why, as a Black woman in this industry, you are worthy of being in this space. And it's like, "What?!" And a lot of times, it's like, "Share with us your trauma and like your triumphs and tribulations and like, give us a long sob story of how you ended up"—and it's just like, why can't you just look at what is? The fact you have to even ask me that question means you acknowledge that I've had to undergo that experience. And usually it's like, like a "special"—no offense, no tea, no shade—BIPOC submission process and you have to do XYZ and blah, blah, blah—that's sharing the trauma, "the blah, blah, blah" And it's like, the documentation is there. The play is there. I'm here.

NA. Right.

MJS. It's either you vibe with my energy or not. I'm going to hold space for you, are you gonna hold space for me? Question mark. But yeah, the whole "proving" thing…I can't. I can't fuck with that.

NA. Yeah.

MJS. If my mom—yeah, can't fuck with that.

NA. She's like "Do I want to curse? Yes, I do."

MJS. Yeah, and then the reason why I phrased it as "proof" versus "documentation" at *that* time—and it's hard to articulate with, like intangible experiences—but the reason I articulated that at that time was because I knew that we, as like a worldwide community, would try to forget what happened.

NA. Aaahh…

MJS. And it's like, "No. This is what happened. Here are documentations of people and what they are feeling"—like, there's not one sort of monolith of feeling that we as the Black women and femme community experience; there are various experiences of this pandemic, you know?

NA. Yeah. On the website, you wrote, "Maybe you went through your greatest joy (*during the pandemic*). We want to record that."

MJS. Yeah.

NA. "Maybe you went through your greatest trauma. I want to hear it."

MJS. Right. It was like a full spectrum of things. I mean, like, personally, my family had a really good time, you know? And, like, it's a privilege to be able to say that; but that's what that was. That's just fact. We got really close. Like, that was Marcus' (*Marissa's younger brother*) last year of high school or something like that? Or like, he was in his senior—whatever it was, I'm forgetting the timeline. And I was expecting to move out. So I was very cognizant of time with family.

NA. Family does seem really important to your work. Like in *Blue Fire* (*and its prequel,* deadbody) you have this intergenerational deathmatch. In *Being Up in Here* there are themes of sisterhood and chosen family. That theme is so present in your work. And it's so distinct and so fun to watch. I think you're really onto something.

MJS. Shout out to the Stamps.

NA. Shout out to the Stamps. Let me see. Do I have one more question? Yeah. For me, the term "Downtown Theater" was really important when I moved to New York City. It was like the artistic movement that I was arriving after. My elders were "Downtown." And the term was always weird to me, because I thought, "We're not even close to downtown Manhattan."

MJS. Yeah...

NA. "We're in Clinton Hill, in Long Island City, in Sunset

Park." But I understood it as an aesthetic. It had become codified. So, Marissa. What are we now?

MJS. What are we now?

NA. When you think about who you are in artistic community with and what you have in common, what name would you give it? Does something come to mind? Do you feel like you're part of a movement, or movements?

MJS. I do. I do feel like I'm part of a movement. I think—I'm also like, "Downtown? We're like…in Bushwick. What are you talking about?" Like, it doesn't add up. Yeah, I don't know what the term is. I *do* think that we fall into the category of Downtown Theater's legacy, but I think that the common thread is that the people making theater under that legacy are disrupters. Disrupters, experimenters, and healers. And like, these are things that I'm borrowing from Deepa Iyer's—

NA. Social change web?

MJS. Map?

> (*Deepa Iyer's Social Change Ecosystem maps 10 different categories of people required for change, including* "disrupters," "experimenters," "healers," "storytellers," *and more.*)

MJS. Yeah. Which has really helped me articulate what am I doing in this ecosystem—because this is not just storytelling, which is one of them.

NA. Yeah.

MJS. I think that a lot of people who just fall under "storytelling" are in commercial spaces—or it's like, that's not where we are. So yeah, I think there's a lot of disruption, experimentation, and healing that's at work in the wake of Downtown Theater.

53rd State Press publishes lucid, challenging, and lively new writing for performance. Our catalog includes new plays as well as scores and notations for interdisciplinary performance, graphic adaptations, and essays on theater and dance. 53rd State Press was founded in 2007 by Karinne Keithley. In 2017, Kate Kremer took on the leadership of the volunteer editorial collective. For more information or to order books, please visit 53rdstatepress.org.

53rd State Press books are represented to the trade by TCG (Theater Communications Group). TCG books are exclusively distributed to the book trade by Consortium Book Sales and Distribution, an Ingram Brand.

LAND & LABOR ACKNOWLEDGMENTS
53rd State Press recognizes that much of the work we publish was first developed and performed on the unceded lands of the Lenape and Canarsie communities. Our books are stored on and shipped from the unceded lands of the Chickasaw, Cherokee, Shawnee, and Yuchi communities. The work that we do draws on natural resources that members of the Indigenous Diaspora have led the way in protecting and caretaking. We are grateful to these Indigenous communities, and commit to supporting Indigenous-led movements working to undo the harms of colonization.

As a press devoted to preserving the ephemeral experiments of the contemporary avant-garde, we recognize with great reverence the work of radical BIPOC artists whose (often uncompensated) experiments have been subject to erasure, appropriation, marginalization, and theft. We commit to amplifying the revolutionary experiments of earlier generations of BIPOC theatermakers, and to publishing, promoting, celebrating, and compensating the BIPOC playwrights and performers revolutionizing the field today.

Fucked + Jolly is made possible by the New York State Council on the Arts with the support of the Office of the Governor and the New York State Legislature.

53rd State Press
new writing for performance

CONTRIBUTORS

Nic Adams
Tristan Allen
Leonie Bell
Eliza Bent
Theresa Buchheister
Ann Marie Dorr
Salomé Egas
Lena Engelstein
Shawn Escarciga
Lisa Fagan
David Greenspan
Ben Holbrook
Hannah Kallenbach
Kate Kremer
Joey Merlo
Nicolás Noreña
Kyoung Park
Cristina Pitter
Lee Rayment
Evan Silver
Sleth
Marissa Joyce Stamps
Cameron Stuart
Christina Tang
Alex Tatarsky
Sanaz B Tennent
Ellpetha Tsivicos
Bailey Williams